The
Holistic Solutions
Workbook

for

Learning to live
Holistically

Vincent John Thompson

The January 2001 edition of the British Medical Journal ran a feature on the subject of alternative medicine and therapy. The overwhelming conclusion to be drawn from the summaries of scientific investigation, doctors' practical experiences and the experience gained from other cultures is that western health professionals need to adopt a more holistic approach to the treatment and prevention of physical, mental and spiritual ill-health. It is a message that the founder of Moss Hill, Vincent John Thompson, was delivering more than 40 years ago and that we continue to deliver today.

Our practice and our expertise have been built slowly and carefully on the strongest of foundations - experience.

It is this experience we now dedicate to you, the reader of this book, created to help you understand and improve your holistic well-being. We invite you to explore our expertise and knowledge to determine for yourself the benefits of living holistically.

The Moss Hill Holistic Centre is set in the heart of North Wales where the Conwy and Machno Rivers plunge to meet each other. The Centre offers a residential facility set in five acres that are totally unspoilt, surrounded by the Snowdonia National Park, an area of outstanding natural beauty. The peace and tranquillity are a welcome relief in the busy lives of our clients.

Dear Reader

This Workbook will help you, whatever your physical well-being or frame of mind at the moment, your life and health can be improved dramatically. However long it took to get into your present situation, if you start living holistically you will feel the benefits almost immediately. If you are already fit and healthy in mind, body and spirit it will remind you of what you already know.

Your age is not important. Wherever you are on life's journey, this book will help you get the most out of the rest of your life, living longer and enjoying your later years. It will show you how to develop yourself as a whole person by considering each part in turn and becoming self-aware. The text will inform, get you thinking or answering questions, all of which will help you. You may wish to purchase a special notebook to record any answers you may give or to set down thoughts or emotions that are generated. Alternatively use the blank pages at the back of the book if you prefer.

The Workbook has three sections, Mind, Body and Spirit. It begins with Mind and includes some searching questions about your earliest memories. This area is especially sensitive. If you find yourself in any difficulty please contact me by using the address or telephone number given at the back of the book or e-mail me at our website

Yours sincerely

Vincent John Thompson

Vincent John Thompson

CONTENTS

Dedicated to the memory
of
FRANK COLLINS

THE HOLISTIC VIEW

Holistic means 'whole', that is all aspects of a person, their mind, their body and their spirit. It may sound a very modern idea but is, in fact, an extremely old doctrine. Some of the principles and techniques are ancient knowledge, based, as now, upon the recognition that we have to look after these three areas equally, that they are interrelated and dependent upon each other.

For example, someone in physical pain will find his or her mind unable to concentrate. They feel tired, agitated and their body chemistry becomes depleted. They are uncoordinated, mentally, physically and emotionally. It is also a fact that if you have suffered an injury, even a small muscle strain, when you are put under mental stress of any kind that area is likely to be aggravated and will result in further pain.

If you are not living in the way that you want to live and have some unsatisfactory or unfulfilled area of your life, this is also likely to cause you physical discomfort. To fill your mind with angry or bitter thoughts will not only show on your face, making you look far older than your years, but will also cause tension which produces pain and may break down your immune system. This could develop eventually into serious illness.

Someone who is spiritually depleted cannot be a 'whole person' either in a holistic sense. If you act in a negative way your personal spirituality cannot help you. Inspiration, help with decision-making, protection and wisdom can all be provided by your spirituality. The spiritual side of you is partly expressed by your conscience and your own morality. It links you with the universe and higher consciousness.

It need not be in a 'religious' sense but beliefs of some kind will help people live longer according to some scientific research. It is necessary for human beings to have some ethics to live by. To be devoid of this could be very depressing and result in physical and mental disharmony and confusion.

It may be appropriate to indulge every so often in a bit of spiritual 'healing' or 'repair' by visiting a supremely beautiful place where the peace and serenity feeds the senses and regenerates us. Sometimes this regeneration happens spontaneously: when you hear some beautiful music, read some poetry or prose that moves you or when you look at a work of art. This is the part of you that feels a magical leap of joy when you welcome a new life into the world or meet someone and fall in love. These experiences go beyond words. They are simply divine. They feed our hungry spirit and provide sustenance as a wonderful memory that will prevent tensions, bitterness and sadness destroying our mind and body at times when life is less than perfect.

Holistic health then, is a harmonious balance of all three: the mind, the body and the spirit. When we speak of a balanced person we mean someone who is respecting all three, who understands that the close interaction between the three means that if one is upset the other two will suffer in some way and that tension will build up.

> *We grow only when we push ourselves beyond what we already know.*

Mind

Healthy Mind

The human mind and human consciousness are still an area of great unsolved scientific mystery. Many unresolved questions exist about the relationship between the mind, the brain and the body. Although much research has, and is, being undertaken, there is still so much to discover. The brain itself is the major organ of the nervous system and is located in the cranium or skull. The seat of thought, speech and emotion, its primary role in humans is as the body's control centre, simultaneously carrying out and regulating the body's day-to-day demands and numerous bodily functions.

As an organ, like the heart or liver, it needs to be healthy, have a good blood supply and the necessary nutrients. It is also subject to physical disease. Indeed some behavioural and emotional problems can be as a direct result of disease or infections of the brain. It can also deteriorate, producing degenerative diseases where functions like memory and movement become affected. The mind operates through the brain in the same way as the breath we take is taken up and used by the lungs. It is involved with 'internal' aspects like memory, feelings, thought and perception and 'external' manifestations like speech, behaviour, intelligence, learning and personality. The science of Psychology has attempted to analyse and understand the mind and its emotions. Numerous theories exist about this highly complex aspect of human beings. What can be said is that personality and individuality are inextricably linked to our minds.

> *"The only irrefutable fact that one can say about oneself is that, I THINK, THEREFORE I AM"*   Descartes

Our thoughts or cognitions are of tremendous importance because they play a vital role in our state of mind and our health. Some people acquire negative thought patterns and emotions and they become a habit and habits are hard to break. They have become the 'norm' and they no longer notice or question them.

To assume this negative pattern of thought, to believe something, a situation, or even a future, cannot be changed may well create a self-fulfilling prophecy. Believing something strongly enough can actually bring it about. If you are thinking holistically you should avoid putting negative thoughts into your mind. Not only can they affect your moods, your relationships, your life at work and play but also your body. Worrying, for example however pressing and serious the problem, does nothing to solve the worry or remove it. At best it creates more tension and erodes your ability to concentrate, think clearly and constructively, to resolve the problem. It blocks the very path we should be following.

> *You use only a fraction of the mind's potential.*

Images of extreme horror and brutality, in films or on television for example, should be avoided if at all possible and any unpleasant pictures that may appear in your mind unbidden should be replaced with calmer, more positive ones. Your mind should be calm and in control unless it is engaged in some necessary mental combat. The power of positive thought should never be underestimated. It removes the limits to your personal potential. It could help you achieve what you may feel at the moment is impossible. You do not have to look far for evidence. The most moving of human stories, the ones that show great courage and eventual triumph, always demonstrate the fact that their survival or success depended upon and used positive thinking to succeed.

Everyone is familiar with the phrases 'run down' or 'down in the dumps'. Both phrases are highly evocative suggesting someone who is physically or mentally depleted, permanently fatigued, prone to infections, needing a 'tonic'. We all accept that our frame of mind affects our health so it should be no surprise that a stressed, unhappy mind is capable of creating a disharmony that results typically in conditions like nausea, asthma, breathlessness, headaches, irritable bowel syndrome, peptic ulcers and certain skin conditions like eczema. These are only initial reactions and can be followed by more serious conditions if the stress and unhappiness continues. We all have genetic weaknesses and it is these that are particularly likely to emerge.

The mind has been shown to be not just the brain but also part of a communication network throughout the brain and the body. It is easy to see how physiology might affect normal mental functioning and vice versa. The immune system uses many of the same molecules as the brain and they are able to communicate with each other. The ability and power of the mind is astonishing. Holistically, all of these factors need to be considered. If you find you are suffering from a headache, stiff neck or backache, for example, and there is no physical injury, it is worth considering the possibility that you have some concerns that are causing tension and therefore pain. Worry, depression, low self-esteem, bitterness or anger not only damages our health, it destroys our potential. If you are in harmony, balanced holistically, illness of any kind is less likely to occur.

The mind has tremendous ability to transmit energy from itself to another mind. When you think towards someone else, and we are doing this more often than people imagine, our energy is transmitted into their energy field. The efficiency with which we receive this energy will depend upon our own level of sensitivity. Although this may appear to be a very special attribute, the fact is that it has its roots in man's early survival instincts and was a necessary skill at that time. To ensure successful hunting and to avoid the dangers of a primitive and hostile world we developed super-sensitivity. This super-sensitivity can be used in a positive way to benefit you in your life today. There is a negative side to this ability, especially if you are highly sensitive. Imagine you are about to have an interview. If the person interviewing you is disinterested in what you have to say you could find yourself unable to express yourself adequately. You could feel, quite justifiably that you had not done your best. By being aware of this possibility you can help yourself combat the negativity.

How might you increase your mind's ability? Firstly, a good balanced diet will feed the brain. Keep your brain exercised doing crosswords or any other brain enhancing and stimulating activity. Reading books and newspapers, keeping abreast of events and taking up new interests and activities will be beneficial. Try meditation, *see page 89.*

In very simple terms, all people start out as little beings with needs that have to be satisfied in order to grow and survive but life's events, experiences and environment can also affect us. If these are painful or unpleasant we develop a defence or defences. This could be symbolised as thickened skin, like a corn on a pressure point on the foot. The kind of defence, the degree of severity, the thickness of the skin created, will depend on many individual factors. This can be either modified or made worse by numerous other circumstances – personality, character traits, environmental issues, position in family, hierarchy, intelligence, health and our own experiences.

These interactions create various guilts and fears, difficulties that when carried on to puberty become overlaid with the complexities of our emerging role as an adult. At this point, there is a great deal of self-discovery, particularly in terms of relationships and the way we perceive ourselves sexually. This is a complicated and vulnerable period and further protective skin thickening is highly likely. This is a time when early unfortunate events and concepts can be reinforced. For example, if someone we love and trust often implies that we are not up to scratch in some way, while we are very young, we are well on the way to believing it.

It is important to remember that all human beings are unique; they all have problems and difficulties, which cannot be avoided. Life is a learning experience, a challenge and full of complexity.

In order to help you on this journey of self-discovery it is necessary that you read the pages that follow. They set out various areas, which may apply to you or prompt you to think deeply about ones that you are unaware of at present. Once you have discovered and acknowledged the areas you would like to explore, you will be self-aware. This is one of the first steps to developing yourself holistically.

A mind that is confused or unhappy about certain issues will create tensions elsewhere in the body.

THE MIND AND THE BODY ARE IRREVOCABLY INTERRELATED

I INTRODUCTION TO SELF DISCOVERY

The following sections under the headings, Environment, Guilt and Fear, deal with how the past may be affecting the person you are today. These are intended as a simple tool to help you. To begin it is necessary to look at them closely. To do otherwise is like trying to apply a fresh coat of paint to a cracked and blistered windowsill, eventually the damaged areas will break through. If you feel you need to take further advice and guidance on these issues it will be possible to do so. Our contact details are at the back of the book.

You may consider that none of these areas apply to you; after all you may feel that you do not suffer from any kind of guilt or fear. Maybe you think you have already explored these issues and you know all about them and their effect on peoples' lives especially your own, BUT do you? People know things intellectually and sometimes instinctively but this does not mean they can act upon or change their thought patterns and responses, just by 'knowing' something. Knowledge needs to be absorbed at a deeper level of understanding. They often say and even argue about something they believe in and yet only live by these beliefs when it suits them, because it is only INTELLECTUALLY that they accept them. By becoming aware of these issues and meditating, you will contact the psychic part of you, the part of you that is at one with ultimate wisdom that knows and recognises the truth and will automatically connect with it in a positive way.

The mind is extremely powerful; it impacts on absolutely every area of our lives. In fact it could be used as a heading for the entire workbook with Body and Spirit as sub-headings. It is woven like a thread through all that we may attempt to achieve with our physical body and has to be used healthily in order to learn to meditate and perceive spirit. We also need to use it to bring about any improvements. It runs through our life and is our means of experiencing, recording and recalling it.

That is why Mind is given priority, right at the beginning of this workbook. As well as being a useful tool, it can also be a block that stands in the way of our development. We need to accentuate everything that is positive in our minds and reduce, or remove the negative as far as it is possible.

Let us see ourselves for a minute as a traveller. We are given at each stage, various parcels and suitcases. Some are light and filled with useful things for the journey, that we can use to make it a more pleasant experience: Food and drink, with enough to share, something to read, a change of clothing and some photographs and their attendant memories, which bring a smile to our face when we are far from home. Perhaps the journey is a difficult one and the nourishment may help us survive when provisions are in short supply. However, the heavy suitcases, full of useless rubbish are merely dragged from one destination to another. They are sometimes piled so high that we cannot see the view, we fall over them and they are so heavy they deplete our energy. They do not sustain us only hinder us. Sometimes they burst open and all the useless contents spill out, causing inconvenience to other travellers and harsh retorts from people whose feet have been bruised by them.

So what is in this detrimental baggage that we are forced to carry? Negative habits, bad experiences, unwanted thoughts, guilt, fear, denial, environmental problems, unhappy memories and confusion. Just think how light and elated you would feel, how carefree if you could rid yourself of all this heavy, useless baggage. Our responses are so affected by the events we have encountered along life's path, that often we cannot see the wood for the trees and in normal circumstances it might take half, or even possibly a whole lifetime to create a clearing that enables us to see ourselves, our situation and find a path we would like to take unhindered by useless baggage. This is an opportunity to clear away the debris, even if is a small amount, unemotionally release yourself from it, put it down, stow it away safely and move forward.

ENVIRONMENT

What is explored in this chapter is our early environment, our earliest experiences, surroundings and circumstances and how they might have affected our adult life. How this helps or hinders us. How with greater understanding we can use this knowledge to improve our lives.

It is necessary to say that if you have experienced a childhood that was traumatic in some way, that involved serious damaging issues, abuse of any kind, extreme poverty, violence, severe mental or physical ill health you should seek local professional help, advice and guidance or make contact with the address at the back of the book. Unless you have already received help it may not be advisable to continue with this particular section at this time. There is much to be gained from the other sections, particularly the meditations that will be beneficial.

The problem with all childhood experiences is that the child, who has nothing with which to compare them, however dysfunctional certain aspects might be, accepts them without question; the child sees them as the 'norm'. It isn't until much later when they are old enough to compare their lives with others that they realise that some aspects of their childhood were unusual. These aspects can be small and relatively unimportant in the scheme of things or far reaching factors that colour the entire life of an individual. Whatever the importance they are most likely to be felt in areas involving their professional life, relationships, or the rearing of children. Whether we consider ourselves more worthy of success than we deserve, or whether conversely we believe ourselves to be less worthy than we deserve, how we handle anger, disappointment and rejection may also have its roots in our earliest years. Reactions can be as varied and as many faceted as individuals themselves. Some will rebel, some become introverted, others anti social or angry. It may even make some more sensitive and caring. It will depend on each individual's personality as to how it will affect him or her.

If you have already had the experience of parenting and feel you may have inadvertently inflicted any of these issues on your offspring, do not feel guilty, it is never too late to make amends and address these problems. Even if your children are now adults.

In order to establish how the following list has impacted on your life in both a positive and negative way it will be necessary for you to work through the headings, which will help revive memories and pinpoint any areas that are, or could be, important. Ignore any that do not apply. For the rest, decide if generally the answer is a negative or positive one or somewhere between. Give yourself time to think and make a note of any that require a longer time to consider more deeply, in your special book or on a blank page at the back. After each question you will find information about how these issues could have affected your life.

1. **The Personalities of your Parents**

    Did you feel loved? Were they both warm, loving, well-balanced, easy going and placid or cold, demanding, aggressive or neurotic? *Feeling loved by warm loving parents helps our development. If your parents had problems you need to redress the balance by acknowledging this and trying to understand and forgive them.*

2. **Your Immediate Family**

    Where are you in the hierarchy? The eldest, the youngest, or in the middle somewhere? Are you an only child, a natural child, an adopted or fostered child? How did you feel towards any brothers or sisters?
    There are advantages and disadvantages in being the eldest. It can force us into premature responsibility, although there are obvious advantages in being the first-born. The youngest or the 'baby' may always be viewed that way. The middle may be the hardest of all the positions. The success of adoption could well depend on how well this is handled. There could well be a 'Why was I rejected' issue. This is where mature, objective understanding regarding the circumstances of the birth parent, will help the individual to overcome these natural difficulties.

3. **The Atmosphere within the Home**

Generally speaking, on average, was it a carefree, happy atmosphere, or was it often one of worry, neurotic behaviour, turbulence and rows?

A happy secure atmosphere where people have a stable and predictable mood is of paramount importance. When turbulence and unpredictability become normal behaviour patterns it can become a kind of security in itself and then discord becomes something that is actively sought in adult life.

4. **How old were your Parents**

Were they young or were they old, either physically or mentally?

Older parents can bring much wisdom and experience to their children but may lack the energy and spontaneity of younger parents. Their attitudes as older parents may inflict a more serious note.

5. **Degree of Care**

Do you feel you were overprotected, was it well-balanced care or were your left to your own devices? Was one parent often or always, absent from the home?

Overprotection can leave us open to a severe shock when we come into contact with the real world. Inadequate protection can produce a street wise and possibly cynical human being. If one parent is missing, the rearing responsibilities will fall on the shoulders of the other one, which can be an unbalanced situation.

6. **Sexuality**

Did your parents help you to feel proud of your body and your gender or not?

For example to be a female in a family that desperately wanted a male, can lead to obvious problems about value. Our bodies and our view of them can be seriously impaired if someone makes us feel ashamed of them in some way.

7. **The Health of the Family**

Generally was the family healthy or was there serious illness, hospitalisation or even the death of one of the members?
Children can often feel guilty if a parent becomes ill or dies. Sometimes they think this could be a punishment for being naughty. Long-term illness in an adult, or their child, can result in a negative and sombre atmosphere. There can also be difficulty in absorbing a long absent member of the family after hospitalisation. Sudden illness can be very traumatic for a child.

8. **Self Confidence**

Were both your parents confident people? Did they manage to make you feel confident about yourself?
Confidence is a true gift that can help in every area of life, parents and other adults can rob children of it so easily. With care it can be reinstated.

9. **Security**

Did you have security when you were young? Alternatively was there a lack of security?
This seems so obvious but children need to feel secure. Parents, who constantly argue, make threats, walk out, even if they return, do not create security. Young children may find it hard to distinguish between what is said in an argument and what happens in reality.

10. **Conversations**

Do you remember conversations as being informative, well balanced with everyone contributing or were they dogmatic? Were you allowed to express yourself freely?
Bubbling, happy, informative conversations are so important. Children need to be able to feel free to express themselves, ask for and receive information. To be cowed or bullied by an opinionated parent on whom they are dependent is a poor start in life and one that may involve fear.

11. Nationality and Culture

Was there a strong sense of who you were, your nationality? Was there lots of culture around or no real cultural nurturing? Were books, newspapers or music in evidence?

Culture provides both identity and inspiration throughout life. It makes a huge contribution to creativity and the enjoyment of the Arts in general.

12. Meals and Foods

Were meals the centre of family life, regular and enjoyable or often missed or of a snack variety?

Meals are part of the expression of love in the family. They provide moments in time in which the family are joining together for a common purpose. It is one of the easiest ways of creating 'family unity'. The absence of 'meal ritual' can lead to poor eating habits and even ill health in the adult.

13. Indulging

Did anyone in the family over indulge in food, smoking, alcohol, drugs or gambling for example?

Addictions of any kind are harmful; serious addictions besides obviously harming the addicted person usually affect at least ten other family members. They could produce many other social problems like poverty or violence and children who have experienced this will be disadvantaged in some way. They may reject the addiction as an adult or follow it; undoubtedly it will have an impact.

14. Financial Situation

Was this adequate for the family's needs? Was there too little money with accompanying worries and tensions or perhaps too much money?

Money is a necessity and older children are inevitably aware of it. Lack of money can be a source of tremendous tensions and the over indulging of children with worldly goods can be equally detrimental.

15. **Abuse**

Did you or anyone in the family suffer physical, verbal, mental or sexual abuse?
Sexual abuse needs special counselling. Help is available and should be sought. Depending on the severity, physical, verbal and mental abuse may also require special help.

16. **Religion and Spiritual Values**

Did they have and engender strong beliefs or did they follow no particular religion?
It is important for children to understand and respect a moral code of some kind and see that their parents adhere to it. They also need to know that other people have views and opinions.

17. **Work**

Was work enjoyed or disliked? Were there long periods of unemployment or was this area very secure?
Our attitude to work can be seriously affected by our childhood experiences. Work takes up so much of our lives that it is preferable for us to find employment, which is both satisfying and interesting for us. Some parents may try to live out their own failed employment desires through their children.

18. **What words would you use to describe your childhood?**

This is a general list designed to get you thinking and your answers may not be as clear-cut as the questions. Write down anything you think is important and that you need to think about further, in your special notebook or in the blank page section.

**ONCE YOU HAVE WORKED THROUGH THE
QUESTIONS IT IS NECESSARY TO
ACKNOWLEDGE ANY THAT
ARE POSITIVE.**

POSITIVE ANSWERS ARE VERY IMPORTANT

If you examine deeply the negative areas of your early life you must also acknowledge the positive ones. They can be used to counteract the less happy memories and are a strong, firm, foundation on which you can build a balanced future. Make a note of them. Use your special notebook or the blank pages at the back.

Now look at any that are negative. It is now up to you to see if some of these issues reflect on the kind of person you are now and if any of the difficulties you experience at the present time are in any way related to these negative areas. If this is the case, you need to explore them in depth, bring your own judgement and experience to bear on them and decide if indeed they are anything more than a passing memory, which you experienced at a formative time.

Some of the questions will not apply to you. Whatever your answers, it is possible to use bad past experiences as a learning opportunity. It is also possible to change any unwanted behaviour patterns. The first step is to become aware of them, to acknowledge them, in order to change them. It is really important not to blame yourself. It is a fact that we may inherit, through our environment, many of our psychological problems via things your parents said to you. These may have affected your view of yourself. Parents will sometimes innocently, but with devastating effect, attribute the child with the same characteristics, often unfortunate ones, of some errant relative.

> *Have you ever noticed how your answer to the same question changes as you grow.*

You are unique: a mix of genetic material and your own soul. Parents naturally exert a great deal of influence over the child's development and many people blame their parents for their own shortcomings in return. It is important to acknowledge that certain behaviour patterns, neurosis and unhelpful habits have been handed down from parent to child. However it is not always possible to blame anyone entirely since so many people have made a contribution.

For example, how your Mother or Father were treated when they were growing up, the events they lived through and any psychological pains they suffered, may have had a direct effect on the relationship they have had with you. Some of these behaviour patterns stretch back into the mists of time through countless generations, it is important to remember that some of these generations lived through wars for example, and other difficult social circumstances. Whatever problems you may have, you need to look at them and do your best to resolve them without laying blame at anyone's feet, least of all your own.

Dislikes you have may be merely someone's opinion, given at a time when you were unable to form your own and which have become a repeated habit. Someone you loved and were dependent upon may have badly let you down because they were unable to cope, for reasons that you might now easily recognise, but couldn't understand at the time. Perhaps the pain of some memories makes you overeat or drink too much alcohol. What is important is to realise that whatever happened, it was not your fault. You were an innocent, vulnerable bystander who literally did not have sufficient experience of life to avert certain situations, or feel able to form and act upon your own opinions. It cannot really be taken away but there is absolutely nothing to feel guilty about. It needs to be acknowledged and a door closed upon it. You may find some of the issues are related to each other; linked together in some way.

By viewing the past with adult eyes and looking at it in perspective as a 'whole', holistically, you will be able to understand and forgive. Our early environments are formative. We have absorbed them like blotting paper, while we were children, failing to question them when we have become adult, simply because they have been stamped with the authority of our parents. Our earliest experiences may be responsible for phobias, fears, dislikes or even hatred and bitterness, which needs to be acknowledged, resolved and accepted. Whatever the reason, however justified, the anger destroys us. It needs to be replaced with insight, understanding and love. Every family has some problems, even the most eminent and powerful families in the country experience difficulties. It is part of the human condition and should be treated as such.

THE HAPPIEST DAYS OF YOUR LIFE?

School is usually the first time we leave our home environment to become part of the wider world. Here we meet people who are not as familiar, who are meeting us for the first time and who are not necessarily kindly disposed towards us. Here we become just one of many other equals, vying for the attention of the adult in charge.

We have to redefine ourselves and our view of ourselves. In the hours we spend at school we are usually a lone representative of our family and background, unprotected by loving parents. It is a coming out, something that many people remember as a stressful experience.

> *The adult we become is influenced by the childhood we have experienced.*

Absolutely anything that sets you apart, where you live, your accent, colour of hair, spectacles, height or weight, can give other children something with which to tease you. If your school did not insist upon the wearing of school uniform there may have been some children who came to school in clothing that was not acceptable to the majority, perhaps because their parents were poor or old fashioned. Free school dinners, if they are not handled sensitively, can make children feel different from the rest. Any one of these issues can lay them open to ridicule and derision. You may have been lucky, but how well we are received at school may not be down to us at all, although it may have affected us deeply at the time. Our background, family reputation, peoples' expectations, both good and bad, can have an affect on us for which we are not responsible.

However the pupils or teachers reacted to you, you can be sure that their behaviour patterns were influenced elsewhere, brought about by their personal experiences and environments, their likes and dislikes, prejudices and desires.

One person in particular may have made life difficult at one of the schools you attended. This might have been one of your first brushes with unfairness particularly if the person in question went unpunished. A percentage of the problems we experience in later life may be as a result of situations and scenarios we experienced during our days at school. In one way or another school has a profound affect on us.

It is, of course, also a fantastic opportunity. Many children experience a release at school, a haven from an unsatisfactory home life; somewhere that offers opportunities that are not available at home, or a stage that can be exploited with many people in the audience (not always exploited wisely either). For some children it is a prison sentence, for others a chance to shine.

What was it for you?
What impression has it left, and does
some aspect of it impact on your life today?

How have you progressed? Is there something you used to enjoy, like Woodwork, Metalwork, Art or Sport that you could benefit from taking up again? If school was a negative experience in your mind, perhaps you should consider **anything positive** it gave you so that you can accept it and lay the experience to rest.

ON THE NEXT PAGE ARE SOME QUESTIONS TO GET YOU
THINKING ABOUT YOUR CHILDHOOD EXPERIENCES
AT SCHOOL. YOU CAN RECORD YOUR ANSWERS
IN YOUR SPECIAL NOTE BOOK OR IN THE
BLANK PAGES AT THE BACK.

On the whole did you enjoy school? Think about each school in turn: infant, primary, junior and senior. Was one school a better, or worse experience than the others?

Did you change schools, because you moved, were unhappy in the school, or because your parents wanted you to go to a more suitable or "better" school? How did the move affect you, particularly in the context of friends you may have had. Did you resent the change or did you prefer the change? What about the other pupils: did they accept you in the new school? Was it easy or hard to make new friends?

Do you remember some teachers with dislike? Think about them now, do you know why you disliked them? Do you remember some teachers with affection? Think about them now, do you know why they were special to you?

Of all the schools you attended which one has the happiest memories and which one the worst? Do you know why?

During your school days did you experience bullying? Were you picked on? How do you think you have coped with this experience? Was it resolved and was the perpetrator punished? When you look back at it now does it still upset you?

What were you good at: sport, art, science, geography, woodwork, maths? Does your employment reflect your strengths? Is there something that you could take up now, as a hobby?

What did you hate most about school?
What did you love most about school?

Remember that bad experiences can have value as a learning tool. Some of the things we see as negative at the time can have a long term strengthening affect, enabling us to deal with these issues more effectively if we come across them again. People can grow emotional muscle, as a direct result of the most awful experiences. Hopefully you will have many positive memories of your schooldays mixed in with the less happy ones.

GUILT

Some people have a tendency to feel guilty about everything.

Guilt that belongs to you is probably best defined as something you have done, of your own free will that you knew was wrong, that you regret and cannot forgive yourself for. Even so, you are probably much less entitled to feel guilty than you think. Most other guilt is inflicted or assumed, often when we are young.

It can happen as the result of not living up to the expectations of our parents and guardians. We could feel guilty especially if we are told repeatedly that we do nothing right. As a result we may develop a need to justify ourselves. The justification may well lead us to seek out, and dwell upon, what we have done wrong, rather than what we have done right. If this attitude is inflicted upon us we can become programmed to fail. We may constantly seek ways to fail in order to have the opportunity to put right the mistakes we have made.

Anything that we do, as children, however innocently, that adults make us feel guilty about, can contribute to long-term guilt. Any subsequent   encounters that touch on this area confirm our worst fears adding further to our already diminished self worth and feelings of guilt. When we are blamed for events that are not our fault, but as a child, we believe they are, we feel guilty. Whatever the cause of our guilt, unjustified and unfounded as it is, if it is accepted or assumed by us, it is carried forward and is extremely destructive.

Quite normal early sexual experiences can leave us both confused and guilty. Any childhood misdemeanour can so easily get us thinking we have done something wrong if too much emphasis is placed upon it.

The handling of any situation, during childhood, that could lead to guilt is crucial. Unfortunately it is often handled in a very clumsy way, which leaves the child feeling guilty.

Adults can programme children to feel guilty by claiming repeatedly that everything, including their own unsatisfactory life is somehow the fault of the child. Sometimes we assume guilt when we are adult. For example, we can feel uncomfortable with our own success, if other members of our family are disadvantaged, in some way.

People who think they are guilty often want to punish themselves and will go to great lengths to do this. For this reason it may be difficult to break out of a cycle of guilt. Meditating can be used to help remove this problem.

The way guilt affects us varies from person to person. It may help to write down not only <u>what</u> you feel guilty about, but also <u>why</u> you think you should be guilty. Use your special notebook or the blank pages at the back.

It is essential that you put your guilt into perspective. Dreadful events happen in the world, some of them brought about by the careless or wanton acts of human beings. Where do you stand in the scheme of things? How serious is your guilt? For example, have you sold drugs or committed genocide? It is important to sort out, what one can be reasonably expected to take responsibility for and what "therefore" you might have a right to be guilty about. This also needs to be put into perspective and in the end, it might transpire that there is nothing to feel guilty about at all.

> *Try not to allow negative thoughts to undermine your health and life.*
>
> *The more you think good thoughts the more easily you will become and stay well.*

FEAR

Fear, the uneasy anticipation of something, is a complex, many faceted subject.

Rational fear is something that we need to keep us safe and in certain situations could actually help us. Irrational fear is different and may come from our very early years when we were helpless and defenceless. It can be reinforced when we face situations that trigger these powerful emotions again. It may be completely unrealistic to feel afraid, we are no longer helpless or defenceless, but we feel the paralysing effects of fear just the same. To carry these fears around can be detrimental to our health.

Many people are natural worriers, they are permanently anxious, often about things that are very unlikely to happen. They have a low tolerance of uncertainty, and change is a fact of life that cannot be avoided. General anxiety on the other hand can be a by-product of stress but it can lead to other, often imagined, fears.

Phobias are fears that can also have their roots in early experiences. Sometimes they are simple and merely inconvenient, like a fear of the dark. Sometimes totally debilitating, like agoraphobia where the sufferer's whole life is brought to a standstill. Other people feel anxious incessantly about minute issues, concentrating on them instead of a bigger picture in which lies their true concern. Harbouring this particular unnecessary fear is nothing more than avoidance.

Fear of the unknown or even believing in superstitions may stop you from moving forward and developing, to a greater or lesser extent. It is a burden, like a physical affliction that has to be coped with on a daily basis. It creates problems, colours your world, distorts your view of things, affecting your work, play, home life and relationships. It can seriously affect your mental health and ultimately even your physical well-being.

All human beings have fears, anxieties and worries from time to time. That is part of the human condition. Our experience and intelligence tell us that life is a series of 'coming outs' from well known and safe frameworks, taking risks and meeting new and exciting challenges, some of which will be more pleasurable than others. Anticipating that they must all be uncomfortable, or even terrible, does not allow us the chance to savour the very essence of life, **CHANGE**. We need to embrace it and use any adverse, disappointing or even painful experiences to learn and develop ourselves further.

Some people who have both the ability and attributes to be successful may not succeed because of a fear of failing, perhaps publicly. Less obvious is the fear of actually succeeding which would involve change; change in lifestyle and social position in both family and community. The opinions of the people around us, what they might think or say about us and whether we ourselves feel deserving of success can be a demotivating factor.

The way we experience fear is highly personal. You can help to externalise any fears you may have by making a list of them. Use your special notebook or the blank pages at the back.

This is also a symbolic act.
Cleaning them out, dusting them off and looking at
them in the cold light of day can be a big step
towards dealing with them. Only then, can
you liberate your potential, move
forward and develop.

> *Thoughts can become a habit, just like behaviour*
> *patterns, so it is important they are*
> *positive rather than negative.*

DENIAL

If you have reached this page and know that there have been questions or possibilities presented to you, which you have either ignored or marked as positive when you know deep down they were negative, you are in denial. In effect it is a misplaced defence mechanism. To deny something is to avoid the truth and replace it with some explanation that is more acceptable. It can involve refusing to accept you are wrong or hiding something that is too painful to remember or admit to.

It prevents you from facing the truth about something in your life that ought to be resolved and integrated into it. Inevitably it has a paralysing effect on getting to grips with problems that hold you back. It may be that you are afraid of appearing foolish, or of being exposed. You may wish to hide some inadequacy or it may simply be a habit into which you have drifted.

Finding excuses for why something is not possible to achieve, dieting successfully or giving up smoking, for example, actually prevents you from succeeding. They may be simple excuses that delay, things like, 'I'll start after Christmas' or 'after the Summer holiday'. More complex ones relate to elaborate facades created to hide the truth, perhaps about a relationship, a loved one's behaviour or the past. Facing the truth is difficult but is something we need to do since not doing so prevents us from achieving and denies us our true potential.

> *We all carry a degree of these problems. That is part of human nature. Understanding them, acknowledging their presence, is the first step to removing them as obstacles to our ultimate potential.*

THE ROLES WE PLAY

In order to make a living, have friends and be liked we have to temper our real feelings and thoughts and to be accepted we have to become, to a certain extent, what other people, our family, our peer group and society want us to be. Or, at least, we need to appear to be what they want us to be.

'Finding yourself' is a popular concept which implies a kind of disembodiment, a separation between the true self and what we may, over the years, become. Our existence has, in a way, forced us all to become something other than our 'true self'. We are like actors confronted by numerous identities that we are required to assume, wearing several masks and so confused in the end that we cannot tell which is the true us, the actor we have to become or even which part we are playing.

Sometimes it is necessary to step back and re-discover yourself, the person behind all the roles you are expected to play to perfection, day in and day out.

Life is a hard struggle. From the cradle to the grave it is difficult, incredible, beautiful but full of obstacles. You need to be able to recognise yourself and your own roles and then use this information to understand others in order to avoid incorrect judgements. The masks themselves can take many forms, worn for very diverse reasons, other than the obvious ones. They can hide identities, cloak serious problems, be foolish, glamorous, or created in order to join and remain in certain social groupings. Teenagers are particularly vulnerable and their desperate attempts to become acceptable to their chosen set will often result in the emergence of someone totally unrecognisable to their family, luckily often on a temporary basis.

It is relatively easy to see the smiling mask of a clown which hides the tears, or recognise the very caricatured mask worn by the character Hyacinth Bucket in the television series 'Keeping up Appearances'. This particular mask is no longer seen by its wearer who has convinced herself, if not others, that she is part of a 'special strata of society' and what is more she has extended this masked role to her entire lifestyle, starting with the pronunciation of her name right down to her household furnishing.

We all wear masks, not just facial masks. They can involve clothing, behaviour, speech and personality. We may have put them on in order to earn a living, to belong, to be accepted or to hide something.

Most of us wear harmless masks. We only use them to help us or protect us and to avoid hurting people around us. What is essential is that you remain true to yourself, know who you really are, what you believe in, even if the public face you present to the world at any given time is a more diplomatic version.

You might ask why do we have to wear masks at all? In effect we don't but not to be masked a little would be like not having a skin. It is protective, particularly in the areas where we are very vulnerable. Most people have observed an aggressive young man who puts over a very hard image, a mask that is both physical and verbal. As a result he may never be actually physically challenged. He is using the spoken word and body language in the same way that some creatures use the ruffling of fur or feathers to enable them to look twice their size and therefore more intimidating.

By practising meditation you can find and be yourself. It offers a refreshing break when you don't have to wear a mask and you are able to be in touch with your true self, your innermost being.

EMOTIONAL STRESS

The situation of human beings in the space of three or four generations has changed dramatically. Our lifestyles and circumstances would be unrecognisable to our great grandparents, particularly the stresses that are part of 21st Century living. Technology has brought tremendous benefits and higher expectations. In the past, human beings only had to bear the sad events of a small community, a handful of people who lived nearby. Now they see and hear the sorrows of the entire world, as they happen, through the television in their own homes. If we are bombarded with images of suffering and deprivation and informed continually about happenings over which we have no control it can lead to additional stress.

From living relatively quiet lives, involved with small numbers of people who are familiar, we now travel, sometimes many miles, to work in areas with which we have no natural affinity and inevitably in so doing brush shoulders with far larger groups, that we hardly know, on a daily basis. Today's lifestyle has brought us higher material rewards, we are more likely to be reasonably financially secure, but the quality time we spend with our families may be diminished. Surviving has been replaced by striving.

The computer age has produced a global community and that is positive. However, where there is a positive there is a negative. Everything we do has a side effect whether negative or positive life in the 21st Century is no exception. The pace at which we live leaves little time to stop and think and the vast amount of information that is taken in by us on a daily basis is staggering. So much in fact that we have no opportunity to filter out the more frustrating, harmful or destructive elements. The expectations of modern life are so great that many people feel under intolerable pressure and strain and is it any wonder?

Following the advice in this workbook will be a panacea for stress. It will enable you to find the still calm centre of your being in the midst of the hustle and bustle of your life.

When we experience mental stress, our emotions are affected and these are extremely difficult to control. We find we have less patience, become irritable or argumentative, which may affect our work or relationships. When our emotions flare up we use and waste a great deal of energy, our judgement is flawed and we may turn to food, alcohol, or other crutches to console ourselves. Anger and frustration can result in physical illness, raised blood pressure, headaches, back and neck pain. Sleeping patterns can become disturbed and we suffer chronic fatigue.

> *What is life if full of care,*
> *we have no time to stop and stare.*

We cannot automatically manage our emotions and it is natural to feel frustrated and angry sometimes. Try to make sure it is totally rational. Let it go as soon as possible. Remember that things are rarely black or white, try not to think in terms of never or always, consider perhaps or maybe. Faced with difficult situations consider them as a challenge, what can you learn from them? When you feel stressed molehills look like mountains, take time out to get things into perspective. Try not to automatically blame someone else, accept that sometimes you will be wrong, we all make mistakes. Forgiving yourself for mistakes, once you admit you're wrong is also very important. Qualify things before you get hot under the collar, assumptions of any kind are dangerous. Try to see situations for what they are, perhaps it is nothing more than an annoyance that you will find hard to remember in a few days time. Keep a note of conflicts:

What was it about?
How did you react?
How could you react differently next time

Further information on stress appears on *page 65*.

Personality

Our identity, our character and how we express it is personal to us. We are a unique mix of genetic material from many sources because so many people have contributed to our existence. We have four grandparents, eight great grandparents, sixteen great, great grandparents and thirty-two great, great, great grandparents! In so few generations the numbers escalate dramatically. Human beings can be introverted or extroverted, solemn or jovial, studious or fun loving, the mix of personalities in both families and communities is part of the rich pattern of life.

Your own particular personality will determine how you respond to situations, to stress and to misfortune. What kind of personality do you have? Are you easy going or fixed in your views? Although it is unlikely that you will be completely A, B, C or D.

A. Is someone who meets challenges head on and can often see a problem before anyone else. They find switching off and relaxing difficult, are 'head' stressed and usually know why they're stressed.

B. Is somebody who appears outwardly calm but has very fixed views. Consequently change of any kind is stressful if it challenges their opinions or work/idea structures. Stressed at an emotional level they just 'feel' upset or stressed without necessarily knowing why.

C. This person is easy going and does not readily admit to ever having stressful situations or problems in their life, although they may exist. They allow other people to take over and are inclined towards giving up too easily.

D. This is someone who just accepts everything, doing nothing to solve or change anything. They just go with the flow. They find making a decision of any kind difficult. They avoid dealing with stress.

> *Perspective needs to be used or it is lost.*

We are all a mixture, but which one of these personalities do you think most closely resembles you and the way you experience stress?

**NONE OF THESE PERSONALITIES IS
RIGHT OR WRONG. THEY ARE ALL IMPORTANT AND
VALUABLE. HOWEVER, THEY CAN ALL
BE IMPROVED WHICH WOULD GIVE
A MORE BALANCED RESULT.**

For example:

A. Would benefit by doing only one job at a time, correctly. Learning to value relaxation more and realising how important social life, friends and family can be.

B. Needs to share responsibility more and realise that others have some ideas and something to offer too. Perhaps by instigating change themselves, they can learn to accept it better and become more flexible.

C. This person needs to find out just who they are, what they believe in and find small goals that are attainable. Finding self-esteem and value will improve their lives beyond all recognition.

D. Needs to practise making a mark and standing by it. Look at the worst that can happen if things go wrong. It isn't necessarily the end of the world.

*The most profound questions in life
are the simplest.*

***Who are you?
Where are you going?***

HOW MANY OF YOU ARE THERE?

- The person you think you are
- How other people see you
- The person you really are

Holistically it would be appropriate to add:

THE PERSON YOU COULD BECOME

We are all so lost in the day-to-day, often frantic, business of existence that unless something serious or wonderful happens we just continue down the same path.

This has been an opportunity to look at yourself: where you began, how you have dealt with the series of 'comings out' that is life and how this has affected your mind and personality.

Some of your behaviour was unconscious in the sense that until it was pointed out you were unaware of it. Once you recognize how you have been reacting, some attempt can be made to put things right. What has occurred is a mind detox. Debris has been cleared away, debris, which stood in the way of your potential and development. A new floor has been put down over the bad experiences. You have been encouraged to celebrate the positive areas of your past while seeing the negative ones as an opportunity to learn something, rather than a way to accumulate bitterness and frustration. These resentments turned inward are very destructive. Their true value is their use to rectify the future. Keep reminding yourself about anything positive that has come out of them. Experiences are an inevitable part of life, like rain they fall on everyone. Try in future to be compassionate to others, even people who appear to have everything, enjoying a perfect and protected life. You know their joys but you do not know their sorrows.

Some people hide their sorrows very well, behind their mask, as we now know. Our own ultimate success may depend on how well we manage to hold on to our identity while conforming and wearing a mask. We need to be able to express ourselves appropriately and carefully. The way we express ourselves can affect the response of the person we are addressing. The way we do this, the way we think and act can change opportunities into dead ends and dead ends into opportunities. There is a need to go on developing the individual within us, to stand tall, express our personality in a constructive way, not allowing our environment, bad experiences, guilt or fear to stand in the way of moving forward. Sometimes the path is blocked and we do not like it. This is understandable because we like to 'have our own way' to survive. The blocked path has to be accepted. Sometimes our desires need to be capped and in retrospect we may come to see that to lose was to win. Not allowing the experience to knot us up or to blame others or ourselves is important. Nor do we need to justify ourselves for our success if we win or succeed. Enjoy it; justifying our position is part of feeling guilty.

Using your special notebook or the blank pages at the back you can record your thoughts at this stage and also express your aspirations for your future.

With your mind in better shape understanding and knowing yourself and others better, you can now proceed to tackling your physical being – your body.

Just as easily as the mind can make you its slave it can set you free.

SELF AWARENESS

REMOVING LIFE'S DETRIMENTAL BAGGAGE IS THE FIRST STEP TOWARDS

Holistic Health

STRESS
WORRIES
PROBLEMS
POOR IMAGE

DENIAL
Can also apply to any
other demotivator. It exists
because one cannot admit to
the real problem and claims it
is 'something else' or a series
of 'something elses'. This is
a very effective long-term
paralyser.

NEGATIVE ENERGY
and
NEGATIVE RESPONSES
Creeps in without anyone
noticing; demotivating
destructive behaviour that
is often infectious.

NEGATIVE
HABITS
When the negative responses
become normal behaviour they
can become habitual. This can
apply to addictions of any kind
that are used as support and
can lead to irresponsible
behaviour.

ILL HEALTH
Can be caused by lack of
exercise and incorrect diet, or
a desire to punish,
(psychosomatic illness).
Alternatively, can be caused by
incorrect outlook, ignorance or
low self-esteem and a lack of
self-love. Carrying guilt, fear
or being negative long
term can also make
one very ill.

GUILT
FEAR
LACK OF
CONFIDENCE

THE PATH TO HOLISTIC SUCCESS

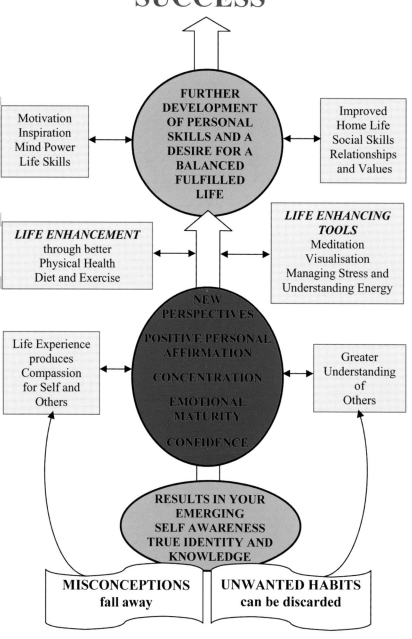

Body

GREAT HEALTH

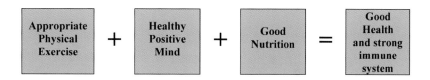

| Appropriate Physical Exercise | + | Healthy Positive Mind | + | Good Nutrition | = | Good Health and strong immune system |

ILL HEALTH

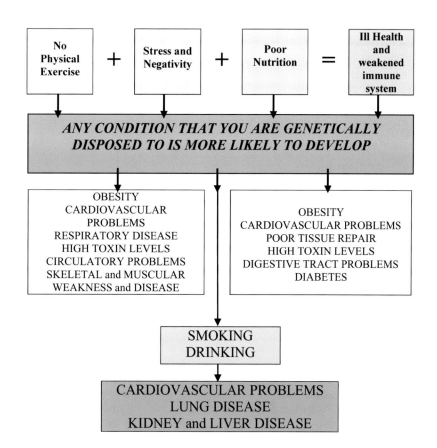

| No Physical Exercise | + | Stress and Negativity | + | Poor Nutrition | = | Ill Health and weakened immune system |

ANY CONDITION THAT YOU ARE GENETICALLY DISPOSED TO IS MORE LIKELY TO DEVELOP

OBESITY
CARDIOVASCULAR PROBLEMS
RESPIRATORY DISEASE
HIGH TOXIN LEVELS
CIRCULATORY PROBLEMS
SKELETAL and MUSCULAR WEAKNESS and DISEASE

OBESITY
CARDIOVASCULAR PROBLEMS
POOR TISSUE REPAIR
HIGH TOXIN LEVELS
DIGESTIVE TRACT PROBLEMS
DIABETES

SMOKING
DRINKING

CARDIOVASCULAR PROBLEMS
LUNG DISEASE
KIDNEY and LIVER DISEASE

NEGATIVE HABITS

We all have goals.
We desire to be happier, healthier or more successful.

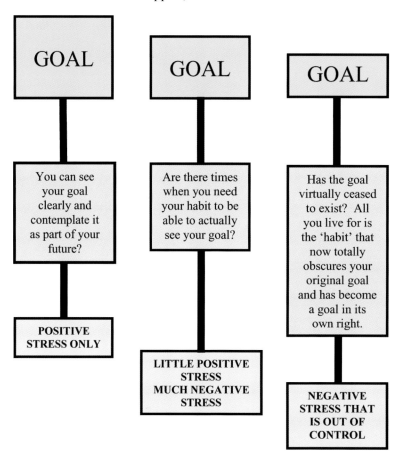

When you are over-stressed it is easy to turn to negative habits to relieve the stress, albeit on a temporary basis. Smoking, alcohol, harmful drugs or over-eating carry a long term legacy that will, even in the short term, be detrimental, affecting your thinking patterns, health, relationships, ability and even future opportunities. Negative habits inevitably obscure our goals.

THE DIET PYRAMID

THESE ARE THE DESIRED PERCENTAGES OF THE FOOD WE EAT EACH DAY

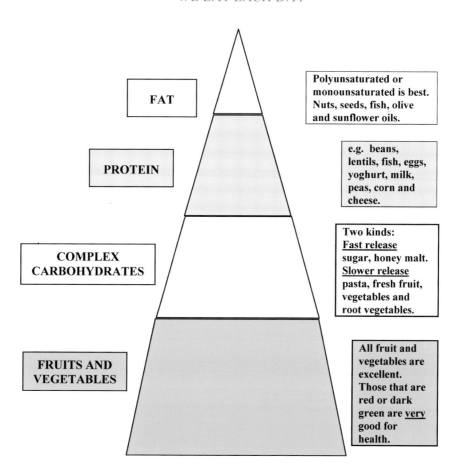

FAT

Polyunsaturated or monounsaturated is best. Nuts, seeds, fish, olive and sunflower oils.

PROTEIN

e.g. beans, lentils, fish, eggs, yoghurt, milk, peas, corn and cheese.

COMPLEX CARBOHYDRATES

**Two kinds:
<u>Fast release</u>
sugar, honey malt.
<u>Slower release</u>
pasta, fresh fruit, vegetables and root vegetables.**

FRUITS AND VEGETABLES

**All fruit and vegetables are excellent.
Those that are red or dark green are <u>very</u> good for health.**

**⅔rds of the body is water. We lose 1.5 litres a day.
Drink 1-2 litres a day if possible, as water,
not always with coffee, tea or squash.**

HEALING FOODS
AT A GLANCE

FOOD	PROPERTIES
Onions, garlic, fish oil, chilli, fruit and vegetables, coffee.	Reduces inflammation of air passages and thins mucus.
Chicken soup, garlic, horseradish, chilli, hot spices, vitamin C-rich Foods.	Thins lung secretions and reduces congestion.
Cranberries, blueberries.	Unique compounds remove bacteria from the bladder.
Cabbage, broccoli, beans, soya, oily fish, wheat bran, olive oil.	Burns up oestrogen so less is available to feed cancers.
Garlic, soya, vegetables, citrus fruit, fish, tea, milk.	Known to stop cancer formation.
Wheat, bran, cabbage, broccoli, cauliflower, milk, yoghurt, seafood.	High levels of fibre can prevent colon cancer developing.
Carrots, broccoli, kale, sweet potatoes, green tea, low-fat milk.	Beta-carotene destroys tumour cells.
Oily fish, olive and walnut oil, fruit and vegetables, flaxseed, onions.	Contain omega-3 oils that halt melanoma growth.
Fruit and vegetables, beans, oats, nuts, olive oil, fish.	Packed with antioxidants and reduces bad cholesterol.
Onions, garlic, cinnamon, beans, lentils, fenugreek, barley, fish, broccoli.	Stimulates insulin activity and regulates blood sugar levels: helpful for diabetics.
Fish, nuts, grains, garlic, olive oil, carrots, spinach, mango.	Keeps blood vessels flexible and free of clots.
Celery, garlic, oily fish, potatoes, avocado, salmon, bananas.	Vitamin C, potassium and calcium are known to lower blood pressure.
Spinach, seafood, pasta, dried beans, cereal, bread, coffee, garlic.	Boosts serotonin levels in the brain so improves mood.
Red peppers, broccoli, kiwi fruit, oranges, cauliflower, strawberries.	Vitamin C makes sperm more fertile.
Vegetables, soya beans, a little alcohol, olive oil.	Contains compounds that help prevent gallstones.
Pineapple, whole grains, seeds, nuts, olive oil, rice.	Calcium helps reduce irritability, cramp and headache during menstruation.
Nuts and fruits, pineapple juice, oily fish, kale, tofu.	Manganese helps strengthen bones.
Oily fish, vegetarian diet, ginger, garlic.	Cytokines that destroy joints are reduced.

Healthy Body

Imagine you have just bought the car of your dreams. This gleaming vehicle is the envy of all your friends, so how would you treat it? It is unlikely you would fill it with diesel if the handbook says unleaded petrol, or forget to top up the oil. Or carelessly scratch it whilst driving continually over rough country it was not intended for, or tie up the exhaust with string if it comes loose. In fact, if the slightest thing goes wrong in the first few months of ownership, you would be contacting the manufacturer demanding satisfaction. You paid good money for it and you know if you don't look after it carefully it will deteriorate very quickly.

Our bodies are free: we don't get a receipt for their purchase and many people never look into the beautiful, efficient and staggering activity that goes on day and night within all of us. We take it all for granted, even the fact that the body, unlike the car, is capable of regeneration. We take it for granted that is, until it goes wrong and then we realise with horror that we actually live in this vehicle and we need it to survive. Some of us starve our body of nutrients, exercise and consideration and are most upset when it begins to malfunction. By thinking and acting in a holistic way you will begin to see your body as a temple, a place in which you reside and that you respect. You will want to give it healthy food so that it can function at an optimum level, exercise it sensibly and generally take care of it.

The holistic view on the care of the body is that it should be looked after in a way that discourages it from breaking down and becoming ill in the first place. However, if there is a problem, which can only be dealt with by using conventional medication, this is, of course, acceptable. There is no intention to discredit conventional medicine, powerful life saving drugs, or surgery when they are needed.

> *Our bodies are free so it is easy to take them for granted.*

After years of cynicism and the rejection of all things 'alternative' the medical profession has begun to seriously consider the benefits of some alternative therapies, especially meditation and have sometimes encouraged their use alongside more conventional treatment. The most encouraging fact is that they are adopting a more 'Holistic' approach. Although there have always been exceptions among medical practitioners, more and more of them are considering their patients as individuals, with individual personalities and involving them increasingly in understanding their illness, its treatment and their eventual recovery. This is the very essence of 'Holistic'.

There are literally thousands of possible alternative therapies: some more conventional and well known than others, some clearly eccentric. It is a market that is growing at an incredible rate. For general help with everyday conditions, if you can find someone who can help you, this is fine. However, it has to be borne in mind that alternative therapists, even more than other professionals, need to be well balanced and have good attitudes towards both themselves and their patients. Holistic in this context means literally that the person intervening on the patient's behalf to try and bring about a positive change, whatever methods they are using, should be holistically healthy themselves. By reading this book you will have the information to make these judgements for yourself.

When someone is confused, unhappy, stressed and unhealthy his or her immune system weakens. This leaves them vulnerable to viral and bacterial infection. What many people do not realise is that we all have genetic weaknesses, malfunction and disease that individually we have a predisposition to develop. When the immune system breaks down any of our personal genetic weaknesses can emerge. Not only does living holistically improve the immune system, it strengthens it.

You will find information on immunity boosting foods on *page 58.*

You will find information on immunity boosting foods on *page 58.*

> *We are what we eat and what we think.*

Eating sensibly is essential for keeping yourself in good health; incorrect diets will always contribute to occupied hospital beds. Most of the supermarkets offer a tempting array of convenience foods, microwaveable, tinned, packaged, ready to eat and often full of hidden additives, preservatives, artificial taste enhancers, salt and colourings, many of which, can and do, have an adverse effect on large numbers of the population. Over the last fifty years there has been a huge increase in the use of sugar.

Manufacturers know that the majority of people have a sweet tooth. When we were young our parents and relatives rewarded us with sweets. Now when we feel upset and need comforting or consoling we turn quite naturally to confectionery. As a result many people, including children, have become overweight and more likely to suffer from high blood pressure and hardening of the arteries as a direct result of eating high sugar content products or junk food, which have a high fat and/or sugar concentration. A diet that includes plenty of fruit and vegetables will keep you healthy. Lots of people mistakenly believe that strength will be lost on this kind of diet. Think about some of the strong animals of the world that live entirely on a vegetarian diet. Vegetables and fruit contain substantial quantities of protein for building strong muscles!

The Government is launching new initiatives to re-educate our tastes in foods, limit public smoking, involve people in exercise and investigate and hopefully reduce, the current trend of binge drinking. The NHS is also vigorously discouraging smoking, which is thankfully becoming increasingly anti-social. Meditation is particularly useful for physical problems, overcoming habits you wish to stop or lowering blood pressure.

You will find an exercise for this on *page 102.*

Our body shape is inherited: how tall or short we are, the colour of our skin, hair and eyes. What is not inherited is its girth or condition. That is determined by two factors. The first is what we eat and the second how much exercise we take. Absolutely every body and every body shape can be improved by eating the correct food in the right quantities and by exercising.

If we are overweight, our heart and skeleton has to carry this around, but strong muscle, carries us. Excess fat is of no value; it is "in effect" stored food and since we are unlikely to suffer a famine, it is of far greater advantage to remove it.

It is not sensible to adopt a fanatical starvation regime to remove fat, rather adopt a sensible eating pattern that reduces the weight over a period of time, reasonably slowly. Start exercising, be active, bike or walk instead of automatically using the car. Take up something that appeals to you that gets you moving - a sport that you enjoy will be more likely to hold your interest for longer than one you don't. Try stretching your limbs gently, in any free moment. Not only is it safe, it is also good for your circulation. In all exercise you need to adopt discretion. Ferocious activity of any kind after years of inactivity is likely to damage you - a jog, for instance on hard ground could damage your knee joints. If you choose this kind of exercise try to do it on soft surfaces like grass or sand rather than on hard tarmac or pavement. Build up to fitness gradually, preferably with some guidance from a professional fitness expert.

> *Be active, bike or walk*
> *instead of automatically*
> *using the car.*

Your local leisure centre, whether run by the local authority or privately, will have promotions and schemes of which you can take advantage and someone to check your general level of fitness to establish what exercises would be most beneficial for you.

One of the best kinds of physical exercise to incorporate into a holistic way of life is Hatha Yoga; they go hand in glove with each other. There are numerous books on the subject and many classes all over the country where you will be supervised. The beauty of Hatha Yoga is that it is not competitive. There are no races to be run and no winners or losers. The pace of the exercises is your own and there are many people world-wide who, in their eighties and nineties, practise Hatha Yoga.

The other area that needs to be considered in order to keep the body fit is sleep. It is a time of regeneration and repair and is absolutely necessary if you are to become and remain a relaxed confident and healthy person. It is not the amount of sleep you need that is important, but the quality of the sleep. Healthy sound sleep leaves you relaxed and looking forward to the day. If you have difficulty sleeping make sure you are not eating a heavy meal before you go to bed, eating fruit or other sugar rich foods. Avoid drinking coffee or tea, because they contain caffeine, which is a stimulant and will keep you awake. If you suffer from insomnia you will find a helpful meditation on *page 100.*

Holistically, value needs to be attached to the body we live in. We need to look at ourselves in a far more compassionate and positive light and look after ourselves physically as well as mentally. Try to use stairs rather than the lift where possible, Consider stretching or using an exercise bike while watching TV and take a break, to walk or stretch, when working on the computer for example.

KEEP A CHECK ON:

o Blood Pressure	o	Cholesterol Levels
o Weight Gain or Loss	o	Alcohol Intake
o Eyesight	o	Hearing
o Blood Sugar levels	o	Skin Condition

Take advantage of any health checks or screening offered by your GP or local Health Authority.

Begin by answering the questionnaire on nutrition overleaf. Come back to it after you have been living holistically for twelve weeks and see just how much your answers have changed.

---

*Think about what you are eating,
food is your body's fuel.*

Nutrition

Please answer the following questions as accurately as you can. Doing so will help you to assess your eating patterns and find the areas that need some adjustment.

How many cooked meals do you eat a day?

One ☐   Two ☐   Three ☐   More ☐

How many snack meals do you eat a day?

One ☐   Two ☐   Three ☐   More ☐

Do you take time to sit down and enjoy your main meal of the day?

Yes ☐   No ☐

Do you eat some fruit each day?

Yes ☐   No ☐

Do you eat some vegetables each day?

Yes ☐   No ☐

Which of these do you drink most a day?

Tea ☐   Coffee ☐   Water ☐   Cola ☐

Squash ☐   Carbonated Drinks ☐   Fruit Juice ☐

How many times a week do you resort to 'fast' food?

Once ☐   Twice ☐   More ☐

Do you take any vitamins or supplements?

Yes ☐   No ☐

Food Glorious Food

WE ARE WHAT WE EAT AND WHAT WE THINK

Inevitably food is of paramount importance and will affect our lives dramatically if we continually starve our bodies of the vitamins, minerals and nutriments that they need. It is our fuel supply; the very cornerstone of healthy living that ensures that both the mind and body have the opportunity to function at the highest levels. Poor diet will create a depleted immune system, obesity and ill health.

What is "good" food? Simple home grown and home-prepared food has been replaced by many, processed, convenience; additive filled and sugar rich alternatives. Altering our diet is one of the easiest changes to make and can have a dramatic effect on health, energy and appearance. Convenience food is often very poor at providing fibre, which is now considered very important in helping to prevent colon cancer.

You should have three 'meals' a day, at least one of which is a 'cooked' meal. Many busy people miss breakfast altogether and are faced mid morning by a low sugar crisis. They reach for what is easily available, chocolate bars or biscuits. Both these products do not give any long-term benefits, just a fleeting burst of energy from the sugar content, with the calorific values stored as fat where they least want it! Bananas are also a pre-packed snack that can be eaten anywhere. Dried figs, dates or apricots are a wonderful alternative to confectionery and come with an impressive list of nutriments. Healthy eating does not mean giving up the tastes you enjoy. It may mean swapping a ready prepared variety to one you prepare for yourself and reading labels more carefully. It may also involve different eating patterns. You should be eating fruit and vegetables every day. Try to resist foods that are high in fats and sugar and replace as much of your shopping basket with organic products as you can. This will ensure you avoid pesticides and other chemical residues that build up in your body as toxins.

Swap full fat dairy products with low fat ones. Eat more fish and nuts. Avoid fast food and processed food except in an absolute emergency. Brown bread, eggs, plain yoghurt, brown rice, seasonal fruits and vegetables are what your body needs: all organic if at all possible. It will reward you well if you provide them.

> ## *Our Diet has a profound effect upon our health.*

Drink plenty of water. Decide to drink filtered or mineral water every day. Water has a cleansing effect on your inner body just as it does on your outer body. Research has shown that if you allow yourself to get too thirsty you may be putting additional strain on your heart. Vitamin and mineral supplements are helpful and are desirable as we grow older, because in later life the body finds it harder to absorb the goodness in food. A full multivitamin tablet a day benefits adults, whatever their age. Meals should also be regular and preferably not eaten in the mid to late evening when its digestion will disturb sleep and encourage weight gain.

Some foods and drinks are stimulants, which are good for us in small quantities. For example, it is better to drink coffee in the morning and tea can be alternated or swapped with green tea. You can add some pure lemon juice to green tea to add the flavour of lemon if you find green tea too bland. The flavoured herbal and fruit teas are available in many varieties and are very palatable. Drinking chocolate is also a stimulant, so avoid it at bedtime. If you wish to drink wine, do so in small quantities, organic varieties are readily available.

> ## *Eat Healthy!*
> ## *Be Healthy!*

Changing your diet is one of the easiest changes you can make. The benefits, when you eat healthy food can be seen and felt very quickly.

Essential Components of a Healthy Diet

Carbohydrates

- o Carbohydrates in the diet, along with fats, provide our bodies with energy, not only to move about, but also for the many processes that are going on within us.
- o Carbohydrates can be found in whole wheat bread, pasta, apples, sweet corn, cereal, baked and red kidney beans, lentils, green peppers, dried apricots, bananas, baked or boiled potatoes, unsalted nuts, dried fruit and brown rice.

Proteins
(You need 1 gram of protein per day per kilo of bodyweight.)

- o Protein is needed to help the body build strong muscles, repair tissues and maintain an effective immune and hormone system.
- o All fruits and vegetables contain proteins.
- o Good plant proteins are peas, beans, grains, lentils, seeds, and potatoes.
- o Animal proteins can be found in meat, poultry, fish, eggs, cheese, butter, milk and yoghurt. Yoghurt releases the energy in food eaten in the same meal.

Fat

- o Some fat is essential in everyone's diet. Foods that contain fats provide not only concentrated energy but also the fat-soluble vitamins A, D, E and K needed for a healthy body and mind.
- o Fish, chicken, vegetable oils, and avocados are good sources of light polyunsaturated or monosaturated fats.
- o Avoid saturated fats as much as possible.

Wonder Foods

VEGETABLES AND FRUIT

Not surprisingly it is recommended that we eat five portions of fruit and vegetables a day. Their value is immense. Apart from providing valuable fibre and many vitamins, they also contain vital components that the body needs to be effective in fighting many diseases and preventing others. This kind of protection is not available anywhere else. If you leave vegetables and fruit out of your diet you are leaving yourself wide open to the possibility of serious problems. Each has its own benefits but generally speaking they can boost our immune system against various cancers, inhibit bacteria, lower cholesterol, protect against eye disease and heal ulcers.

For example, the humble parsnip contains no less than six anti-cancer agents; onions, which are probably the oldest medicine, are full of antibiotics, can prevent blood clots and stomach ulcers. Potatoes can help lower blood pressure and are useful in relieving some rheumatism. Lettuce contains silicon, a component of collagen, for joints, arteries and connective tissue. Celery not only soothes the stomach, it can actually reduce stress hormones. People with kidney problems, fluid retention or ulcers will find celery juice very helpful. Eating avocados can help male fertility. They also guard against some cancers, help blood pressure and stabilise blood fats. Avocados are also cholesterol free, although they do have calories.

Broccoli and brussels sprouts are super foods. They are full of antioxidants and one of the most effective foods to guard against cancers. They regulate insulin levels, are good for anaemia, boost energy and are an anti-stress, vegetable. The old wives tale about carrots is true. They do protect the eyesight and the arteries and protect against smoking related cancers. Beetroot, like many red vegetables, is very good for you, fighting infections, removing toxins, stabilising body acid, aiding tissue regeneration and fighting inflammation of the bowel.

Apples are good for your heart and as the saying goes, they 'keep the doctor away' as people who eat them regularly are said to have fewer colds and other respiratory complaints. Apples also bind themselves to any pollutants in the system and thereby remove them. Blackcurrants are the richest source of Vitamin C. They boost immunity, protect against cancer and help with throat infections.

Grapefruit is an excellent detoxifier. It helps the body resist the growth of tumours, heals wounds, aids digestion, relieves constipation and boosts energy. This is truly an impressive list and it is the only citrus fruit that can help with inflammatory conditions. Other citrus fruit is best avoided if you have an inflammatory condition. (The juice of the grapefruit can also react with some prescribed drugs so check with your GP or pharmacist). Cherries can guard against gout, help prevent blood clots and can relieve the pain of both osteo and rheumatoid arthritis. Bananas are energy boosting, "anti-stress" and stimulate digestion. They are excellent too, for relieving pre-menstrual tension as they produce a 'feel good' factor when eaten.

It would be possible to fill another page with fruits and vegetables – rhubarb, pineapple, melon, grapes, kiwi fruit, marrow, beans, peppers, tomatoes etc, and every one of them would contain truly beneficial qualities that you cannot afford to do without. It is really important to include them in your diet. Buy them as fresh as possible; organically grown or perhaps you could consider growing them for yourself?

Try to eat five portions of fruit and vegetables per day

Holistic Dieting

The most important thing in successful dieting is the way you

THINK.

Although this appears in the Body section nearly every other section in this book will help you lose weight. Quite simply, if you eat more calories than you need or expend, you will store them as fat. So what has thinking got to do with it? To successfully diet you will need to do a lot of thinking, first about **WHY** you eat too much and second about why you cannot succeed, despite innumerable books and magazine articles that guarantee success in weeks!

Here are some of the most common statements people make about why they find it difficult to succeed:

> ► I come from a long line of big eaters
> ► My partner/family like me the way I am
> ► I've always eaten the same amount
> ► I carry a lot of water
> ► I've got big bones
> ► I've got problems with my glands
> ► My whole family is big
> ► I've always had a sweet tooth

Maybe you like food and like the sensation of feeling full. Maybe it's a habit that has crept up on you and your body and mind now expect it. Possibly you are too tired and exhausted to be bothered, or you eat to comfort yourself. When you were young your parents gave you treats when you were upset or faced something unpleasant, or rewarded you with sweets when things went well. Only you will know what the reason is, but there will be a reason, even if it is only that you do not care any more about carrying around too much weight, being uncomfortable, finding it hard to find clothes that fit and knowing that one day it may hospitalise you.

FIND THE REASON

Frustration, anger, low self-esteem, depression, bereavement, disappointment, feeling unloved can all contribute. You are the only person on this earth that can help you to diet and keep you eating sensibly and healthily. Consequently you have to **WANT** to diet find a diet, that appeals to you and **follow it**. Of course you can lose weight. It will take time and you will need to work out why you eat incorrectly first. You also need to avoid starving yourself. Eat every 4 hours; even if it's only a piece of fruit otherwise your metabolism will slow down. Also drink water; it will help detoxify your system.

Reward yourself each time you lose weight; buy yourself something nice other than food. Start looking at the clothes you are going to be able to wear when you have lost weight; provide yourself with a new image and a new **attitude**. Start to exercise. Before you know it you will see the results, use visualisation to help you. *See page 88.*

HEALTHY IDEAS TO TRY

o   Cut down on sugar and salt.
o   Eat plenty of fresh vegetables and fruit.
o   Drink plenty of water each day.
o   Drink tea, coffee and alcohol moderately.
o   Eat calmly and eat every four hours or so.
o   Avoid eating too late at night.
o   Avoid skipping meals.
o   Put some of the ritual back into eating make it special.
o   Consider what you are about to eat, use a special bowl or plate, and try using a smaller one to help lose weight.
o   Choose organic chocolate for iron and lack of additives.
o   Swap sweets or chocolate for a banana, apple, mandarin, dried apricots or prunes, for example.
o   Try to avoid fast food.
o   Cook food from scratch. Fresh ingredients do not necessarily take longer to cook.
o   Eat more salads (organic is best).
o   Swap meat for fish – it also cooks faster!
o   Try whole grain bread and cereals.
o   Replace cakes and biscuits with fruit.

Exercise for Health

To stay looking young some of us spend many hours and hundreds of pounds improving our appearance and looking at our faces for signs of ageing. If we exercised and improved our physical health, creating suppleness and youthful movement it would make it far harder for someone to guess our age.

In the past, most human beings had to do more physically. Many occupations involved manual labour. There were no cars to transport them and walking was much more part of life than it is now. They did not have the endless labour saving machines that we are blessed with and survival often depended on being reasonably fit and active. It would not be surprising to find that many people today can and do 'take it easy'. The human body is designed for movement. Modern life unfortunately, does not encourage this and as a result many people have become overweight and unfit. If you exercise you can expect to live longer and enjoy life more. That is a fact that has been established by countless studies in recent years. No one is suggesting the need to become a fitness fanatic but you do need to introduce a moderate amount of exercise into your life and do it regularly. If you have already done this you will know just how beneficial this can be. If you are over 30 this is absolutely essential, especially if you are leading the average, highly stressed modern life and resort to overeating, drinking or smoking in order to cope.

A middle aged man is three times more likely to suffer a heart attack if he doesn't exercise than if he does, and for women exercise can help stop the development of brittle bone disease, osteoporosis, in later life.

Get Fit – Live Longer!

If you have not exercised for years do not rush into strenuous exercise routines overnight. Start by walking short distances each day and doing some stretching exercises. If you plan to take up more demanding pursuits have a medical check first and build up to it slowly. Joining a fitness club where you will receive professional advice and guidance is sensible. Try to adapt whatever exercise you decide to take up so that it fits into your lifestyle easily.

It is not necessary to start playing a demanding sport every day. It needs to be a simple and effective exercise initially, especially if you are going to keep it up over a long period. For instance – do you take every opportunity to do anything energetic during the day? e.g. climb stairs rather than take a lift; walk to the bus or train? Each of us has different interests, capabilities and strengths. What type of exercise will your body best respond to? Most importantly why are you going to exercise? Obviously to get fit, but do you want to improve cardio muscular function, change your body shape, become more flexible or develop muscular strength? You have more chance of success if MOST IMPORTANTLY you enjoy the exercise you have chosen and especially if it allows you to measure your increased levels of fitness as you progress.

Exercise benefits not only the body but also the mind and the emotions. It can have a positive mood enhancing effect, releasing stress and clearing the mind. It also uses energy to create more energy. It improves posture, flexibility and balance. No one can deny the wonderful tingling in your body that comes from exercise, especially when you haven't done this for a long time.

Exercise benefits not only the body but also the mind!

It would be possible to fill this workbook entirely with all the exercises or sports you could embark on, there are so many to choose from. You as an individual need to make your own choices and decisions about what sport to take up based upon your present level of fitness and what you want to achieve. You may wish to take up something again that you have enjoyed in the past or just do some gentle physical activity like dancing, for example, which combines leisure and social interests with getting fitter. Whatever programme you decide upon, it needs to be balanced, effective and progressive in some way. It will be individually chosen by you but needs to be tailored and monitored, especially if you have been a couch potato for some time. Hopefully, you can find something that is intellectually stimulating in a way that provides you with a challenge and some historical or statistical background that you can explore.

At the present time 70% of men and 80% of women are not sufficiently active to benefit their health. If they were, nearly one third of coronary heart disease could be avoided; a quarter of the people over forty five with non-insulin dependent type two diabetes just wouldn't have this problem and just over one half of hip fractures in this age group wouldn't have happened. Exercise improves bone density, maintains body weight, reduces stress and improves mood and self-esteem. What are you waiting for? It is essential for a balanced, holistic lifestyle.

Arguing for your limitations will inevitably create them.

Are You Stressed?

Stress is the adverse reaction people have to excessive or unwanted pressures or any other demands placed upon them. Reasonable pressure and challenge can be both stimulating and motivating to some people. This is positive stress. If we develop stress that is in response to demands we cannot cope with it is negative stress.

Stress can take many forms and we do not always recognise when we have become stressed. The symptoms could include any of the following: -

PHYSICAL	BEHAVIOURAL
o Inability to relax o Chronic fatigue o Frequent headaches o Poor immune system o Dizziness o Shortness of breath o Weight gain or loss o Digestive problems o Changes in eating habits o Backaches o Muscle tension anywhere including neck/shoulders o High blood pressure o Increased perspiration o Skin problems and rashes o Insomnia o Depression o Hair loss	o Poor decision making o Decline in work performance o Impulsive emotional behaviour o Erratic or poor timekeeping o Frequent absenteeism o Poor interrelationships with others o Accident-prone o Over indulgence in smoking food alcohol or drugs o Lack of pride or interest in personal appearance o Nail biting o Disinterest, lethargy

What can make you stressed in your Personal Life?

o   Any combination of work and personal matters that leave an individual feeling they cannot cope adequately.

o   Inability to cope or deal with problems associated with early life or environments.

o   Changes of any kind, i.e. divorce, marriage, illness, bereavement, family problems, relationships, financial worries, additions to the family, sexual problems, mid-life crises, holidays, moving home, teenage or elderly dependants.

o   Physical or psychological illness. This can be the cause of stress or a symptom of it.

o   Addictions, phobias or any dependency, in self or family.

o   Uncertainty, especially about the future.

o   Lack of appreciation from other family members.

o   Financial worries.

o   Poor environment or living conditions.

MEDITATING can help **DIMINISH** the *debilitating impact of stress on your life.*

What can make you stressed in the Working Environment?

o <u>Change</u>. Restructuring, re-organisation, altered personal role. Changes in technological applications or methods.

o <u>Harassment</u> or any kind of victimisation.

o <u>Lack of control</u> over content of work or the pace of work.

o <u>Poor communication</u>: work relationships with little feedback or acknowledgement of work competence. Minimal consultation.

o <u>Insufficient training</u> or promotional opportunities.

o <u>The way work is organised</u>. For example: too much, and too little work or responsibility. Inflexible work schedules, unrealistic schedules, unstructured work objectives or deadlines. Conflicting or confusing demands.

o <u>Long hours</u>. Not being able to complete work in time available.

o <u>Poor working conditions</u>: Lighting, noise, temperature, workspace.

Recognising stress is the first step to dealing with it.

How does your Body react to Stress?

Dr Hans Selye, in his pioneering work at the University of Montreal, defined the physiological stress response. It starts when the stressor event triggers the nervous system, which signals the adrenal and pituitary glands. These glands produce the hormones ACTH, cortisone and cortisol, which stimulate protective bodily reactions:

o   The blood flow is redirected to the muscles and the brain

o   The heart beat increases

o   Glucose and fatty acids enter the bloodstream to provide energy for the body

o   Our senses are sharpened which increases our alertness

This response called the "FIGHT or FLIGHT" response was a necessary one for our primitive ancestors. When they encountered a wild beast, it gave them the energy to either fight back or flee.

It can still be appropriate in today's world, when we are faced with a challenging situation but many of the situations we face on a day-to-day basis, sitting in a traffic jam or a stressful interview, for example, give us the same rush of excess hormones with no way to release them. After you have been challenged, you need the time to recover. Your body needs to digest the glucose and fatty acids in the bloodstream, relax and build up an energy supply for the next stressful situation. If there is too much stress, or if it lasts too long, or you are continuously in a stressful situation, your body will not be able to relax and restore the balance.

This will impact, for example, on your intellectual capacities. You may be absent-minded, have difficulty concentrating, forget easily, have a lack of creativity, or be more indecisive. Paying attention to the signals your body sends out will help you.

Massage for Health

Since earliest times human beings have reached out to touch. They have used their hands to give comfort, warmth and healing to each other. It is a simple way of communicating; touching is contact, an affirmation that we are not alone, that we have value. Although you may not be aware of it, you reach out and touch in a comforting sense every day, when you rub an injured knee, smooth a fevered brow or take someone's hand. It is easy to see just how valuable 'touching' can be. Massage is based on this natural human instinct.

Our skin which is our largest and most sensitive organ, registers our sense of touch. Skin arises from the same cell layer as the nervous system in the embryo and as such is the "external" portion of the nervous system. `Millions of nerve endings run throughout the body, they control much of the way it functions. Through certain massage techniques these nerve endings can be soothed or stimulated. Touch is so powerful it can soothe both the body and the mind.

Intensive care wards have testified to the fact that patients in a coma have recovered more quickly when they are stroked and touched regularly. It has been established that massage is a natural tranquilliser as it encourages the production of endorphins, which are a natural 'morphine within', not only does this reduce pain it also produces feelings of euphoria. Stroking the body reduces heart rate and lowers blood pressure, it calms. Headaches, backache, stomach cramps and PMT all respond well to massage. It can help release blocked emotions as you feel more valued and aware of your body. It stimulates the tissues promoting healing and regeneration and most importantly restores balance. Since so much of ill health has its roots in our stressful way of life and the strain it puts upon us, it is easy to see how massage that combines warmth, support and natural de-stressing is so successful at warding off ill health.

It is also suitable for all age groups, from babies to pensioners. Children and adults who have a disability, or who cannot be communicated with in the usual ways, using speech or sight, for example, find massage highly acceptable and very beneficial.

Through our skin we feel and thereby experience physical 'reality'. It is how we receive certain sensory messages, it let's us know what we need, whether we are hot or cold and what is happening in the atmosphere and environment around us. It provides vital information for our survival. It is also a means of communicating with our interior. It is a fact that calming and smoothing our skin will calm and soothe our insides.

This is also another starting point for self-discovery and an essential aspect of self-awareness. To be holistically aware you need to explore your reality, your flesh and bones, not merely ideas and concepts, but the part of you that is alive, that you feel, in a physical sense. Massage gives you an ideal opportunity to become more aware of your body. Through massage you will learn to listen to it, treat it with respect and automatically, naturally, change any negative habits that could be damaging to it. You will want to take care of it, feed it correctly and exercise it regularly.

> *We have solutions, we just need to recognise them.*

Massage can be used to increase performance in sport by aiding recovery and alleviating the painful side effects of fatigue after strenuous physical activity. When you start to exercise lactic and carbonic acids appear in the muscles and the surrounding tissue. These are waste products and lactic acid, which is an irritant, causes pain. It is formed when glycogen, which is stored in the liver and the muscles, is burned during exercise and has to be reconverted back to sugar and stored again, or drained into the lymphatic system and eventually carried out of the body. Any stiffness after strenuous prolonged exercise can be removed by stimulating the metabolic process with massage. This can also help people who wish to lose weight or who feel sluggish and lethargic.

Repetitive strain injury, fatigue, insomnia and cellulite can be improved when massage is given. It is the quickest, single, most effective way, to produce a state of relaxation and remove stress, by soothing the nerves.

Many doctors recommend massage. Scientific research has proven beyond doubt that it is effective in many areas and has far reaching benefits. In the early 1900's Chapin, Knox and Brennemann carried out studies on babies who had been, for some reason, institutionalised and had therefore experienced less tactile stimulation than children cared for by their mothers at home. These infants were less well developed both physically and mentally. Also a far higher percentage died in infancy than would have been expected in the population generally.

In the 1950s and 60s a group of scientists carried out similar experiments on some small mammals, some being handled and stroked repeatedly while others were not. Of the two groups the ones that had been stroked and handled had better immune systems, higher fertility and appeared less stressed that the others.

> *Massage is one of the quickest ways to create a feeling of well being.*

There are many books available so you can learn to give massage and this is something to consider if you have a partner and would like to learn how to give and receive this together.

Many colleges of Further Education also have massage courses and if you do not want to follow a course they will undoubtedly offer massage to anyone who consents to being a 'client' for an hour. All health spas, many beauty salons, some sports and leisure centres offer massage often combined with other treatments.

When you have the benefit of good health you need to maintain it and touch, in the form of massage, can also be a way of preventing illness.

IT IS SO EASY TO GET CAUGHT UP IN
STRIVING, ACCOMPLISHING AND
CONFORMING THAT WE BECOME
MIND ORIENTATED AND OUT
OF TOUCH WITH OUR BODIES.

Massage gives you the opportunity to focus
on and listen to your physical needs, to the
reality of your body.

Massage and Rebalancing

The human body can become easily 'unbalanced' and massage is
particularly good at rebalancing because it stimulates the energy
flow. These energies flow freely when you are balanced and in
harmony. Most people have experienced that leaden feeling in the
stomach when something goes seriously wrong. Some people can
feel their blocked energy when they sit quietly by themselves
perhaps before meditating. An area inside feels dark and heavy,
inert rather than satisfied. This feeling denotes that the energy flow
has been interrupted. The energy itself has become negative.
Created by thought patterns like worry, fear, sadness, revenge, self-
pity or resentment which have been held on to, frozen inside. This
causes tension and creates disharmony within the body preventing
the energy from flowing freely.

This is mentioned here because in one way it is the link between
the physical body, which is seen and the unseen aspect of the body,
which relates to the spiritual.

EXERCISE

Please answer the following questions by ticking the relevant boxes. Doing so will enable you to assess your current attitude to exercise and find any area that needs adjustment.

| Do you attend a gym? | Never ☐ | Weekly ☐ | More often ☐ |

| Do you take part in any sport regularly? | Yes ☐ | No ☐ |

Do you do any of the following?

| Walking ☐ | Swimming ☐ | Cycling ☐ | Running ☐ | Golf ☐ |

| Do you sometimes walk instead of using a car? | Yes ☐ | No ☐ |

| Do you sometimes cycle instead of using a car? | Yes ☐ | No ☐ |

What do you do to relax?

| Watch Sport ☐ | Read ☐ | Watch TV ☐ | Hobbies ☐ | Socialising ☐ | Theatre/Film ☐ |

| Would you like to be fitter? | Yes ☐ | No ☐ |

| Would you like to lose weight? | Yes ☐ | No ☐ |

Your answers will tell you what you need to do to become fitter and possibly provide a few suggestions about how you might to this.

IDEAS FOR EXERCISE

Always warm up before exercising
Do not exercise directly after eating
Exercise on a regular basis

POSSIBLE EXERCISE	DESCRIPTION / BENEFITS
Stretching	▸ Do this before you get out of bed in the morning. ▸ Mimic a cat.
Hatha Yoga	▸ Calming for mind and body. ▸ Increases flexibility and mobility.
Stretching (calisthenics)	▸ Involves excellent breathing techniques and gentle stretching.
Walking	▸ Uses the whole body keeping it supple and healthy. ▸ Excellent way to start getting fit.
Swimming	▸ Removes stress and tension from entire body including the facial muscles. ▸ Good for cardiovascular health.
Fitness Programme **Cycling (can be on an exercise bike)** **Aerobics (high and low impact)**	▸ Increases self-esteem and self-image. ▸ Can be tailored to suit you personally. ▸ Gives a natural high as it releases endorphins in the brain. ▸ Increases metabolic rate and produces a strong cardiovascular system. ▸ Results in a high level of physical fitness. ▸ Helps depression and stress.

If you make the important decision to become fitter and healthier,
visualise the new you that you are going to
achieve in a few months.

Spirit

PREPARATION FOR MEDITATION

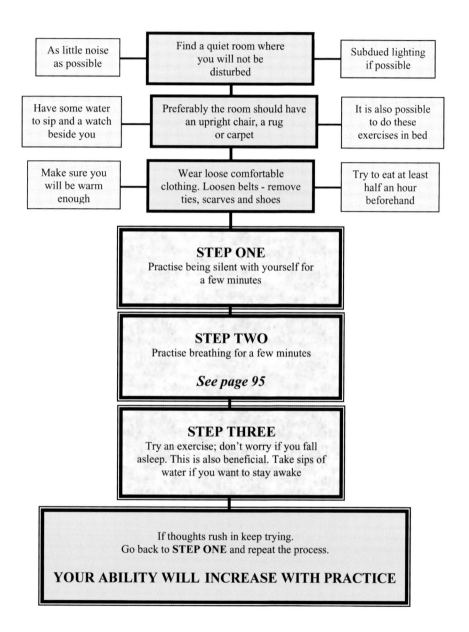

As little noise as possible

Find a quiet room where you will not be disturbed

Subdued lighting if possible

Have some water to sip and a watch beside you

Preferably the room should have an upright chair, a rug or carpet

It is also possible to do these exercises in bed

Make sure you will be warm enough

Wear loose comfortable clothing. Loosen belts - remove ties, scarves and shoes

Try to eat at least half an hour beforehand

STEP ONE
Practise being silent with yourself for a few minutes

STEP TWO
Practise breathing for a few minutes

See page 95

STEP THREE
Try an exercise; don't worry if you fall asleep. This is also beneficial. Take sips of water if you want to stay awake

If thoughts rush in keep trying.
Go back to **STEP ONE** and repeat the process.

YOUR ABILITY WILL INCREASE WITH PRACTICE

COLOUR AWARENESS

Colour awareness can help us to rise to a higher level of consciousness. It is also possible to use colour as a meditation exercise. The colours are listed below, with details of the properties they possess

Meditations using colour are on *pages 97, 98, 100, 101, 103, 104.*

COLOUR CHART	
RED	For giving energy for physical activity, such as any kind of work or sport.
YELLOW	To activate the mind on an intellectual level, when studying for examinations, learning or resolving problems.
ORANGE	For love and wisdom. A highly spiritual colour, which also helps with the understanding and appreciation of music.
PALE GREEN	For people suffering from insomnia, nervous tension or frustration, it will also make you more sympathetic and relaxed.
BLUE	For philosophy, group healing and self-healing. It unites the mind and spirit and helps with the burdens of responsibility.
INDIGO	For calming, stress reduction, self-healing and spiritual healing.
VIOLET	A colour that helps with the understanding of the cosmic energies, for love, spiritual attunement and true knowledge.
WHITE	For pure concentration. White contains the properties of all the colours.
PINK	Soothes the nervous system. Increases love energy to assist healing. Changes negative thinking to positive. Can repair physical or mental injury.

COLOUR VISUALISATION

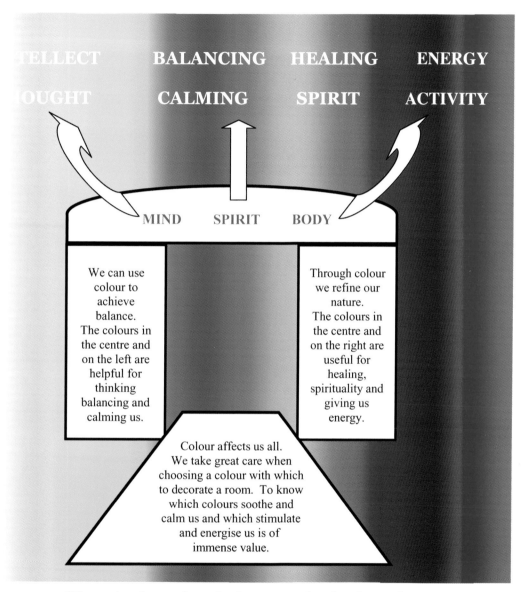

When using these colours for decor remember that these colours can be diluted with white to produce a paler colour or made into a darker colour, they will still retain some of their basic properties.

THE CENTRES

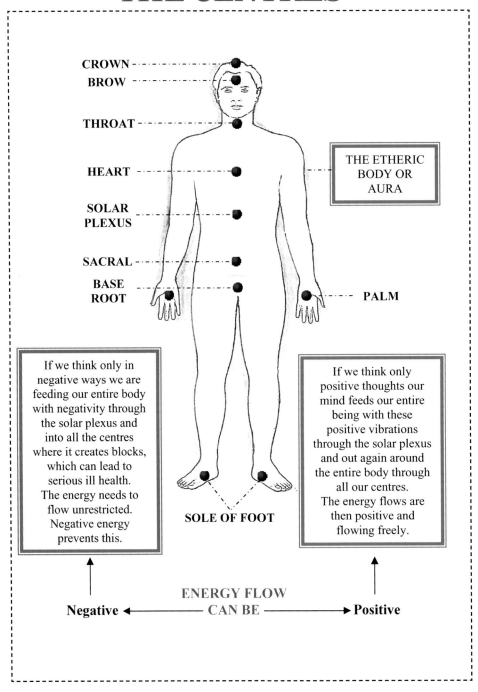

CROWN

BROW

THROAT

HEART

SOLAR
PLEXUS

SACRAL

BASE
ROOT

THE ETHERIC
BODY OR
AURA

PALM

SOLE OF FOOT

If we think only in
negative ways we are
feeding our entire body
with negativity through
the solar plexus and
into all the centres
where it creates blocks,
which can lead to
serious ill health.
The energy needs to
flow unrestricted.
Negative energy
prevents this.

If we think only
positive thoughts our
mind feeds our entire
being with these
positive vibrations
through the solar plexus
and out again around
the entire body through
all our centres.
The energy flows are
then positive and
flowing freely.

ENERGY FLOW
CAN BE

Negative ← → Positive

SPIRIT

We live in a society that consumes and all of us are consuming material goods. We live in a material world. We need these items but they should serve us, not rule us. Many people live solely to acquire them - the latest mobile phone, television or car - all of which come and go in and out of fashion, finally ending up in a scrap yard or rubbish tip of some kind. This part of your workbook deals with what is enduring, your inner person, your spiritual, eternal self. Many people do not even acknowledge this aspect of their being. It is kept in darkness, as a prisoner, just as having a beautiful piece of art and keeping it under lock and key in a dark cupboard might be, a precious object, not allowed to shine, never nurtured or shared and in a way, undervalued.

Reference has been made, on a number of occasions, to higher consciousness. This may be a term with which you are unfamiliar. It refers to a state of mind that is beyond selfish desires. Thinking about the welfare of other human beings, although they may be people you will never know or meet. Having care and concern for the planet and the welfare of all living things upon it, in the way that you might care for your own family. Higher consciousness is the expression of your inner self.

This part of you, unlike your physical body, is indestructible. It has insight into the truth and has psychic abilities; it can help you to enrich your life. How do you find this beautiful ethereal eternal part of yourself and start developing your own personal higher consciousness? By becoming aware of its presence, meditating and refusing to focus continually on what is transient and illusory.

Stressful situations, emotional problems and overwork prevent us from relaxing naturally and a release is sought in superficial experiences and over-indulgences, often in pleasures that are short-lived and in the long term extremely harmful.

The inner self desires both meaning and harmony so the unsuccessful search produces more negative stress, which drives us on to further indulgence to try to fill the devastating emptiness inside. A lifestyle needs to be developed that can be integrated into the individual's deeper nature, one that is balanced to satisfy both the inner and outer self. Denying our inner self prevents us from realising our full potential. It seems hidden from us, as if behind a veil, something we are one day going to investigate.

It need not be like that. In this section you will discover how you can restore balance, become calmer, remove stress and have a more positive attitude. If you need energy or the strength to deal successfully with difficult distressing events, either in the past, the present or the future, the reserves needed will be made available.

The veil will be lifted and you will feel as if you have awakened from a sleep. Your life will feel more immediate and vital. You will as a result, be able to generate sources of energy that until now have not been available. You will also understand how to prepare and programme yourself using visualisation, which is a meditational tool that enables you to use your rediscovered spiritual self to create confidence and banish any tendency you may have to expect a gloomy and negative outcome to any coming situation. Even seemingly hopeless scenarios can be improved if you are prepared to give a little time to visualisation. You will also find it useful if you have repeatedly and unsuccessfully tried to give up an unwanted habit. By using visualisation you can succeed. More information about visualisation appears on *page 88.*

In the 1960s and 70s the word 'vibes' was very popular. It referred to the vibrations given off by the cells in our bodies and everything around us. The vibrational frequency varied depending on the individual and the environment in question. For example, when one person comes into contact with another, and their vibrational qualities are similar, the reaction may be like that between two magnets drawn to each other. There may be an emotional attraction, with the two people feeling that they have known each other all their lives and they may discover that they have a lot of similar interests.

This is partly how communities are formed, because most people in families and other social structures are of the same level of spiritual development, their vibrations are similar and they share mutual interests.

On the other hand, people functioning on differing levels give out vibrations to each other that are unfamiliar and they feel ill at ease in their presence. These vibrations are being sensed when people enter houses or other buildings that they've never visited before and experience an immediate dislike to their surroundings. They may describe them as 'unfriendly' or 'uninviting'. What they are actually receiving in their mind is a field of radiating energy that has been left behind by other peoples' presence, their vibrations.

You can test your ability to sense vibrations by observing how you feel in differing locations. For example, accommodation where people have been enjoying themselves, like a holiday chalet, has a very relaxed atmosphere and happy positive vibrations. The bedroom usually occupied by children is even more relaxed and happy because unlike their parents they do not bring any problems or worries whatsoever with them! However, if you meditate you can expect to find yourself thinking positively automatically all the time, not just on holiday. Joy in life, looking forward to tomorrow, while enjoying everything life has to offer today, is natural. And if your life has become anything else, it needs serious restoration. Life is precious and should never be reduced to mere existence. Meditation reverses all negative trends.

The meditation exercises are the central hub to all this new activity simply because at these times you are at one with yourself, in total harmony with your emotions and the experience. The mind, body and spirit are aligned in a state of pure bliss. Even if at the time you are unaware of it. Let us begin to find that still, pure centre of your being – your spirit.

> *Use the Spirit within creatively, as an artist, to make living an Art.*

ENERGY

By living – being alive, we create energy within ourselves. It flows around us internally and is also emitted from us. Human beings and all other living things, animals, birds and insects generate this energy, although the frequencies created vary substantially with each species. This energy also exists and is emanating from all vegetation, the seas and the earth itself. Everything is vibrating and emitting energy. This vibrational quality needs to be positive in human beings, flowing uncluttered, in the way it might be when we are perfectly healthy, happy and in a meditational state. This is why meditation is so important in this context. Life is, as we know, full of frustrating, difficult situations and experiences all of which cause us to malfunction vibrationally. A comparison could be made to a church bell. When it is hanging normally in the bell tower it can produce the most beautiful clear ringing note. If it becomes entangled with anything and its resonance is affected, so that it cannot vibrate correctly, the wonderful sound is lost and is replaced by a tuneless one. When you are an uncluttered vessel you vibrate correctly. Anger, frustration, worry and ill health can all prevent the body from vibrating correctly. This bio energy field is known as the Aura. There are in fact a number of energy bands around us but what we are referring to here is what is known more accurately as the etheric body which is projecting from the physical body. It is vibrating at above the speed of light and therefore cannot be seen by most people.

Some people may find this information hard to assimilate. As they are unable to see vibrations or the Aura for themselves, with their own eyes, they might doubt their existence. In much the same way as a Victorian gentleman might have viewed the possibility of a man walking on the moon or the possibility of television. A box that showed coloured moving images!

It seems unfamiliar and extremely unlikely although surprisingly many ancient civilisations knew about the Aura and representations of it and references to it, have been made in both art and culture, for thousands of years, by unconnected civilisations across the globe.

Until 1939 there was no technology capable of proving its presence, so science did not accept its existence, until in Russia Senyon Kirlian accidentally rediscovered a high voltage, high frequency method of photography that exposed a corona of energy as an image around biological specimens that had never been scientifically recorded before, thus proving its existence. These findings were published eventually in 1960. Kirlian photography has proved that there is a kind of etheric blueprint, in terms of energy around all living things and if some part of the original is missing, as in an amputated finger or the missing part of a leaf, for instance, its original bio energy field will still be seen as complete, recreating the image as it was before the part was removed.

There are people who have the ability to see the etheric body and can gain considerable information about that person's overall physical condition and mental attitude from its pattern, colour or colours. The etheric body or aura is part of a structure that processes the life force, allowing us to absorb and use it, through the main centres in the energy system of the body. These centres or focal points need to be open, clear and uncluttered in order that this energy can flow around us. It is possible to use the mind, particularly during meditation, or massage as already mentioned, to encourage this flow, which can become blocked because of mental or physical problems, which in turn create further 'blocks'. Our inner systems crave balance and harmony and may tell us if there is a problem by expressing it as tension or pain in or near these focal points or centres. There are connecting channels between all the centres that virtually follow the nervous and vascular system of the body so it is easy to see how its malfunction will have a profound and progressive effect.

Since many of us do not know of the existence of this invisible system, we can do little to help it.

We need to understand how this is as important as keeping our veins clear in order that blood flows through them. Not realising that the invisible system is able to take up, generate and process energy, that we can use, in the same way as the lungs take up breath to oxygenate our whole body, we are missing out.

Energy is at our disposal. We are free to use it wisely, conserve it or waste it. Consider for a moment that, after sleeping, you begin each day with a reserve of energy. As the day passes that energy is expended on physical, mental and emotional activities, according to your responsibilities and the choices you make. It is inevitable that you will sometimes, maybe often, use up your energies unwisely. Even professional athletes who prepare meticulously for sporting events can get it wrong. Over training can cause depletion in energy levels and its flow, which may lead to injury or mental and emotional fatigue. Similarly, how many successful people are there who have not learned how to use their energy correctly. Who after meteoric rise to fame find they cannot sustain the energy needed to maintain their success and try to redress the balance with an unhelpful habit that leads only to ultimate failure?

Taking part in exercise, being happy, eating a healthy diet and meditating all help to increase our energy levels, whereas anger, disagreements and worry, all part of our hectic disharmonious lives, can fritter our energy away in enormous quantities.

Contrast these examples with a young, happy child. Free from the clutter, confusion, anxieties and pressures that we experience as adults, they instinctively understand how to use their energies to enjoy themselves.

> *We are free to use our energies wisely or to merely fritter them away.*

Their choices are simple and their boundless reserves of energy carry them through the day to a deep and contented sleep. They have used their energy to its full potential. They have an uncluttered flow.

When we are young we have tremendous reserves of energy. Life has not taken its toll of us and until our mid twenties most of us are able to live life to the limit, without noticeable depletion. If we compare our inner energy to that of a rechargeable battery, it gradually runs down and as we grow older the recharging process becomes less effective. Some old people have almost ceased to recharge and find it difficult to gather together enough energy to complete the most mundane of tasks, whether physical or mental.

We have the ability to be aware of our energy and despite all the frustrations of daily living and growing older; we can learn to rebalance it, keeping our batteries fully charged, by meditating. Fifteen minutes of meditation is more beneficial than many hours of disturbed sleep. In a meditational state you are calming your entire body and opening any blocked energy channels, allowing yourself the opportunity to recharge yourself efficiently, naturally removing any unwanted impulses or negative thoughts and allowing your mind to control your entire being. When you are vibrating correctly and your energy flows are positive and not restricted you are healthier and more able to achieve your ambitions. Living holistically will automatically keep your battery fully charged and create balanced positive energy that your etheric body craves.

The value of positive energy cannot be over estimated. Its presence and its correct use and understanding are supremely beneficial to the Mind, Body and Spirit.

> *Our Inner Systems crave*
> *Balance and Harmony.*

VISUALISATION

Human beings are blessed with creativity, to a greater or lesser extent we are all able to use our imagination. Visualisation is a way of using this ability, to resolve problems and create confidence, particularity in situations, which might otherwise be filled with anxiety. It is also a way of thinking about your life in a positive light.

To explain this, let us consider for a minute the role of an architect. Having received a brief to design a house. He or she will use all their technical skills, together with their knowledge of the needs of the potential occupier and overlay these with their imagination. He or she will visualise the finished house and then set about putting this into plans that the contractor can interpret, the blueprint. When you use visualisation as a tool, you will be creating personal blueprints that you can follow to improve your life. You are probably already using visualisation, when did you last "rehearse" an important interview in your head, imagining the responses? When you are facing a situation in which you desire to do as well as you possibly can and succeed, you leave nothing to chance. If you believe that visualisation of a coming event, can help influence the outcome and make you more relaxed, why not use it regularly in your life?

Visualisation can be used to re-programme your responses, for example, if you have just started to diet, it is helpful to put images of yourself as you wish to become into your mind. You can also use visualisation to help avoid the coffee, cream and sugar you usually succumb to at 11am. Imagine yourself in the same situation as usual, but replace the coffee with a glass of water. See the glass in front of you, filled with clear water, slightly frosting the sides of the glass and looking very inviting, lift it to your lips, imagine the cool clean water on your tongue. Apply this formula to any situation; just arrange the situation to increase the likelihood of your success. Only use visualisation for positive outcomes. You can create the future you desire, success, achievement and the attainment of your personal goals by using visualisation.

MEDITATION

The definition of Meditation is to exercise the mind in contemplation. Finding your way to the calm, still centre of your being, using the powers of your own mind to concentrate and control your thoughts, thereby calming both your mind and body, bringing normally unconscious actions, such as breathing, under your control. Without drugs, it induces a tranquil state that refreshes and purifies the mind, creating self-awareness and relaxing all parts of the body. It is a respite that can be taken whenever most needed that will restore balance, will and peace, imparting the ability to manage both stress and problems.

Meditation will help you discover that part of you that is often lost in the day-to-day process of living. By meditating you will automatically lift the burden of unwanted habits, thoughts and outgrown experiences, remove negative conditioning and purify your inner self, while giving rest to the parts of yourself that never rest.

Most people give themselves to their family, friends and occupation, losing themselves in their responsibilities. By meditating you will rediscover yourself and develop your human potential, enabling you to devote your time and energy with greater ability to whatever is at hand, committing yourself more fully to your vocation or retirement, expressing yourself more accurately, radiating love and health outward, each hour each day. You will come to understand your thoughts, feelings and emotions as never before, directing them in a positive way for good.

These brief interludes of mental retreat will induce moments of great calm and benefit your entire being.

By meditating you will learn to improve your lifestyle and your mental and physical condition, thereby enabling you to live a fuller life in every sense of the word. You will learn to revitalise your inner being and generate new sources of positive energy. These are natural abilities that are lying dormant within you at the moment.

As our lives unfold we have many experiences, we learn so much, but much of this learning process is painful and leaves scars that prevent us from using our experience to any real advantage. When you begin to meditate you shed the burdens and the scars fade. It is like being born again, seeing life in a new light, just as it was when you were young, but still retaining all the wisdom and experience you have gained over the years.

SOME OF THE BENEFITS
Of
MEDITATING

By meditating both concentration and memory are greatly improved and the ageing process is slowed down. Meditation is a great comfort to older people and ideally suited to them because of its sedentary nature. It also provides positive help during bereavement. If you are fortunate enough to enjoy good health, learning to meditate will help you to maintain this happy state of affairs. Good health is one of the more obvious rewards of meditating. Scientists have managed to demonstrate the effect of meditation on the physical body, which becomes more efficient in a meditative state.

> *As an individual you must learn to master yourself with discipline and patience.*
>
> *Learn to master your senses, instead of being enslaved by your passions, emotions and habits.*

Blood pressure is normalised, lactate levels in the blood are reduced, breathing patterns are slower and deeper, while metabolic rate is lower than during actual sleep. Perhaps the most interesting fact is that brain patterns become more relaxed, although mental alertness is maintained. Even young sportsmen and women who have bodies in peak condition find that meditating can produce superhuman reserves and endurance. There are schools that use meditation as part of the curriculum. They have claimed a far higher percentage of exam successes at higher grades than other schools and have also experienced a reduction in instances of bullying.

Stress-related conditions, such as insomnia, high blood pressure, irritable bowel syndrome, migraines, asthma and PMT, have been shown to benefit from meditation, and many people believe it has helped them give up the alcohol, smoking and tranquillisers that were ruining their lives. Research from around the world supports these claims, and doctors too, are singing its praises. On average people who meditate visit their doctor 50% less than those who don't. Thousands of British Doctors recommend meditation.

You have your own master within, your own conscience and personal morality, your life force, which is your link with higher consciousness. By meditating you will be taking a positive step to using your thoughts and actions in a divine way, enabling you to go beyond negative wants and desires, and a state of mere survival, into the higher realms of consciousness. It will enable you to become a pure channel. It will eventually be like opening a door and allowing higher consciousness and the cosmic energies to be transmitted through you whenever you need them. Remember that the same power that placed the planets in the universe is available to you; it can be channelled to flow through you, simply by meditating.

- **HARNESSING YOUR ENERGY**

  Many business people find that they can conserve and use their energy more effectively when they practise meditation. Within all of us is a huge untapped reservoir of dynamic energy. It is known as the vital life force, which you can use in a natural way to dispel tension and anxiety. By meditating you will learn how to harness this energy, to be calm and clear headed, able to utilise the energy just when you need it, in much the same way as martial art techniques use energy, using it effectively and powerfully to gain the desired result.

- **SPORT**

  Anyone who meditates will experience increased performance in sporting activities. Meditation is currently being used by top sports people of the world to achieve perfection.

- **REDUCING DRINK, DRUG AND CIGARETTE DEPENDENCY**

  A recent study found meditation to be three times more effective than anything else in treating alcohol, smoking and drug addiction.

- **WELL-BEING**

  Meditation induces higher knowledge and inner tranquillity. Answers to problems manifest themselves; deeper levels of consciousness are made available automatically

- **KEEPING YOU YOUNG**

  Meditation may be the easiest way to stay young. One group of 50 year-old meditators who had been practising meditation over five years were shown to be as fit and healthy as the average 38 year-old. Other studies have also shown that people who meditate regularly are likely to live longer.

- ## REGULATING BLOOD PRESSURE
  ## AND IMPROVING HEART HEALTH

  High blood pressure paves the way for stroke and coronary heart disease. A recent American study found that meditation reduced blood pressure by a level similar to that produced by drug therapy. Meditation can aid heart conditions including palpitations and angina as successfully as drugs. A 1987 study found that meditators had an 87% less heart disease hospitalisation rate than people who were not meditators. Meditation gives rest to parts of the anatomy that otherwise never rest, even in sleep. It strengthens the immune system and enables the body to recover quickly after injury or illness.

- ## REDUCING STRESS

  As a major cause of ill health, stress can directly cause panic attacks, anxiety and depression and is related to many other problems. A recent study showed that 20 out of 27 stressed-out volunteers improved significantly following an eight-week course of meditation.

- ## BOOSTING MEMORY AND CONCENTRATION

  Many business people are aware that their success rests on thinking clearly and to be able to do this it is essential to rest the mind. Practising meditation can help the work obsessed to switch off and relax at the end of a stressful day

- ## MAKING YOU HAPPIER AND BRIGHTER

  Meditators feel less irritable; less depressed and have an undeniable feeling of self-worth. Meditation also improves memory, creativity, productivity, efficiency and energy levels. Students practising meditation were shown to increase their IQ by five points in two years.

PREPARATION

Whatever your age you have the ability to meditate. No special attributes or expensive equipment are required. When you begin to learn to meditate it is essential that you choose a quiet room. Initially, environmental factors are very important. As you progress you will be able to substitute other locations, perhaps even in the open air, eventually being able to meditate anywhere.

The room you choose should have a comfortable upright chair and a rug or carpet to lie on. You can use whichever you prefer. There should be no distracting sounds or bright lighting. Nothing should distract the senses, the temperature should be comfortable, the lighting subdued and noise of any kind kept to an absolute minimum, if silence proves to be impossible. You should be dressed comfortably, loosen any tight clothing and remove anything restrictive; belts, ties, scarves, shoes and, if the room is warm enough, you may also wish to remove socks, stockings or tights.

Set aside fifteen minutes and ensure you will not be disturbed in your chosen room. To begin with just be with yourself silently for a few minutes at a time, whenever you have the opportunity. Move on, when you are ready, to any of the meditation exercises. Plan to do at least one of them a day for a minimum of ten minutes, unless stated otherwise. Your ability will improve with time, discipline and patience. Thoughts may rush in. This is natural and to be expected, at this stage. Try to empty your mind of the day's issues and events. In time, the process will become easier. Accept, to begin with, that you are attempting and achieving complete relaxation. This in itself has many benefits. Do not worry if you fall asleep, this is also beneficial. If you want to discourage it, take a few sips of water from time to time. The level of relaxation will increase naturally and there will be progression to full meditation. Remember to return to these instructions if you need to. Don't give up; it may take a little time.

BREATHING

The following two meditations use breathing as a focus. Correct breathing is of tremendous importance. Although many people never give breathing a second thought.

Life is a breath and the absence of it is death. We live as long as we breathe and we breathe as long as we live. Our life starts with the first breath and ends with the last one. We never stop breathing whether we are awake or asleep. Without air we cannot exist. It is one of the most important sources of nourishment. The condition of our skin, bones, teeth, hair and nails depends partly on the oxygenated quality of our bloodstream.

All the activities of our body, from digestion to creative thinking need an oxygen supply. It is amazing therefore, that most people never think of taking a few deep breaths in the morning, although it is as important as a bath, shower or breakfast. Furthermore, however good the breakfast and however well we digest it, it is useless without that essential supply of oxygen.

Deep rhythmical breathing is a useful exercise to precede meditation or relaxation. It nourishes and helps to cleanse the body and build up its resistance to attack by disease. It also calms the mind, the emotions and the nervous system. If you have heart or lung disease it is advisable not to do deep breathing. However, anyone capable of normal exercise will find this most beneficial. This exercise is also very useful before sleeping.

Sit in your comfortable chair. Take a few deep breaths, inhaling through the nose and exhaling through the mouth. Do these four or five times and then continue breathing normally

> *Peaceful outflowing breath carries both light and energy to every cell in the body.*

MEDITATION USING BREATHING

After you have done the previous exercise three or four times, you can progress to taking a deep breath and holding it while you concentrate on each part of your body in turn. This will develop and increase the objective as well as the subjective consciousness in each part of your body. This process will awaken the nerve centres in these parts, until, by the time you have reached your head you will find that your whole body is tingling with life and vitality, such as you have never experienced before.

Deep breathing means inhaling (breathing in) but not to the point of discomfort. Then hold the breath for a few seconds without discomfort, and exhale as instructed. For instance, when you come to your feet, hold a deep breath while you concentrate on the left one, and then exhale through the nose. When you come to concentrate on the right foot, take a deep breath through your nose again as before, then exhale through your nose. You will find that this adds to your vitality. The deep breath gives you an extra amount of positive energy, which further quickens the subjective senses of those parts on which you are concentrating. The blood in its circulation at those points discharges the extra vitality, that enters the blood cells of the lungs each time you take a deep breath and hold it, where you are concentrating. You are feeding each of these points with an extra amount of vital life force, which includes the very essence of the physical and mental power that is required to awaken their subjective centres.

If there is anywhere in your body that is tense, inhale a deep breath and breathe out again slowly, and keep on doing so for a few minutes whilst you concentrate on the tenseness.

A CENTERING
MEDITATION

Sit relaxed in a chair. Take a few deep breaths, concentrate on the breath, calm the mind and breathe. Feel the calm of a tranquil lake, with no ripples upon it, now breathe normally. Centre your concentration on the middle of your forehead.

When you have achieved this, extend your concentration to visualize a blue circle around you, four feet away from you. When you feel you have achieved enough concentration visualise another blue circle three feet away from you. Do this for a few minutes. Take a few deep breaths, and then breathe normally. Now visualize a blue circle around you only a foot away from you.

After doing this to the best of your ability, take a few more deep breaths, and then breathe normally again. Now bring your concentration to the middle of your forehead and concentrate on you, find your inner self and for a few minutes be at peace with yourself.

You may repeat this exercise again using a golden yellow coloured circle and then again using a pure white one.

There is a past which is gone forever but there is a future which is still our own.

CANDLE MEDITATION

A plain white candle, placed in a safe candlestick provides a meditation that will help your concentration and create harmony in your mind and body.

Place the candle somewhere safe at eye level approximately one metre away from the chair in which you have chosen to sit. Take a few deep breaths and then, breathing normally, concentrate on the flame of the candle. Around the candle flame you will see a colour. As you relax the colour or colours will clear and the halo of the flame will become white. All the time, repeat the word 'love' or 'peace' gently in your head. Once you can do this you will have increased your ability to concentrate and created harmony within yourself.

Once you have mastered this exercise you will be able to change the colour of the candle's halo at will, to any colour of your choice, by using pure concentration.

Use the light of the candle flame to create a light in your inner self. Allow the light to grow until it suffuses your entire being.

MUSCLE RELAXING
MEDITATION

Go to your chosen room and settle in your chair or lie on the floor, whichever is the more comfortable. If you are going to use the floor, make sure that the room is free of draughts. Close your eyes. Clear your mind.

Focus your mind on your muscles, beginning at your feet and gradually working up your body progressing to your face and head. Keeping your muscles relaxed, breathe through your nose. Become aware of your breathing, focus on its rhythm and, as you breathe out, say the word 'love' repeatedly in your head for two minutes. When the two minutes have elapsed, spend a further two minutes running your mind over every muscle in your body, mentally relaxing and smoothing each one in turn.

Approximately ten minutes from when you began the exercise open your eyes to check the time. Do not use an alarm clock or timer, but place a watch or clock conveniently nearby.

> *Let go of the word LOVE,*
> *allow it to melt into your aura,*
> *create a golden white light around*
> *you with each peaceful breath,*
> *relaxing every muscle.*

A HOLISTIC MEDITATION

This meditation is particularly useful for anyone suffering from insomnia. It can be done lying on a bed or actually in bed before going to sleep. Begin by thinking into each part of your body - starting at your toes and working upwards, but only one leg at a time and one arm at a time. Imagine you are massaging yourself, smoothing and calming each part of you. Do this slowly and do not worry about how well you are doing it, or if you are doing it correctly. Just relax and concentrate. When you have completed the mental massage of your entire being, visualise you are bathing in a blue light such that your body is completely covered and surrounded in a blue light - a blue that is the colour of a beautiful clear sky on a summer's day.

Continue now by choosing one and only one, of the following visualisations, whichever you prefer.

❖ Imagine you are in a beautiful garden on a warm summer's day. You can hear the birds singing from the branches of a magnificent tree above you, through which the sun is streaming. All around you is the perfume of flowers. You can see them in perfect detail, the lovely colours and the shapes of the velvety petals.

❖ Imagine you are barefoot on a golden beach, the soft sand under your feet, the waves lapping gently and the seagulls calling overhead from a cloudless blue sky. You can feel the gentle warmth of the sun on your back, as you walk along.

❖ Imagine you are looking over a vast still lake at a towering mountain range on a warm summer's night. The sky is crystal clear with millions of stars for as far as you can see and the moonlight shines brilliantly across the shimmering water. The gentlest of breezes touches your face and you relax into the harmony and wonder of nature.

EXERCISE FOR IMPROVING CONCENTRATION

Good concentration plays a very important part in our daily lives. Accidents in the home, at work and on the roads are often caused by lack of concentration.

This exercise is helpful in the evening or just before retiring as it may make you drowsy for a while after completing it.

Choose an A4 piece of paper in white or any one of the colours given in the colour section that is appropriate. Choose a healing or calming colour if it is to be used before you go to bed.

Fix the sheet of paper to a wall. This should be level with your eyes when you are seated. Place the chair six feet or 2 metres away from the sheet of paper. Do not allow any other thoughts to come into your mind; concentrate on the colour itself. To begin with, do this for a maximum of two or three minutes at a time and take intervals in between to relax, ignoring the colour. Then return to concentrating on it. Do this for not more than ten minutes in total.

> *All the colours of the rainbow can be used for meditation and relaxation.*
>
> *By using the correct colour for your needs, allowing it to suffuse your entire body, you can bring harmony to every cell of your being.*

AN EXERCISE
TO REDUCE HIGH BLOOD
PRESSURE

To begin, drink a glass of cold water whilst sitting in a comfortable chair and relax completely. Having done this, concentrate your thoughts on your heart. Tell it to beat more slowly for a few minutes. At the same time, use your concentration and tell yourself that your blood pressure will be reduced. After holding this thought for about five minutes, you will find yourself becoming cooler. Take a deep breath, as deep as possible, through your nose, with the mouth closed. Hold the breath for just a few seconds and then exhale through your nose. This will change the air in the lungs and will have an additional beneficial effect upon the blood pressure.

You should do this, if you have eaten a heavy meal just before going to bed, so that your blood pressure will be improved before you go to sleep for the night. (It is far better to avoid having a heavy meal before going to bed. Try to eat at least three hours before retiring).

All meditational exercises in the course will improve the health of anyone suffering from high blood pressure.

> *When you, the air and the*
> *water of the lake are quite still,*
> *you can see the best reflection.*

A MEDITATION TO ASSIST HEALING

When friends and relations become ill it is natural for us to want to 'do something' to help. This meditation gives you the opportunity to send some healing energy to the person concerned wherever they are.

If you are closely involved you will also need to set aside time for your own meditating, as the care of a loved one who is ill, can be very debilitating. If you remain in good spirits you will be more effective in all the areas that will be demanded of you.

During your usual meditation session visualise the person who is ill, send loving, positive thoughts towards them. Now imagine that you are placing a gentle, pink cloud around them, bathe them in the cloud, and surround them with it. Do this for five minutes.

By doing this exercise you will be transmitting positive, healing energy to their etheric body.

> *Deep peace of the Running Wave to you*
> *Deep peace of the Flowing Air to you*
> *Deep peace of the Quiet Earth to you*
> *Deep peace of the Shining Stars to you.*

THE VITAL FORCE WATER MEDITATION

The following meditation uses water as a focus. Water has a very calming and healing influence on the mind and body. We subconsciously associate it with cleansing and baptism, together with a feeling of safety when we were suspended in water in our mother's womb. Taking off our clothes and entering water makes us feel we have shed our heavy load and are as children again. Bathing and swimming are immensely beneficial, especially to those who have restricted or painful movement on dry land. It provides a happy release, a release that we all feel to some extent when we relax into a fragrant, warm bath, or take a shower.

The healing influence of water is well documented. The following exercise has been developed over 40 years of researching the beneficial properties of water and meditation and it utilises the natural healing influence of both.

Select a special glass tumbler and use this tumbler each time you do this exercise. Fill the tumbler with water. Find your comfortable chair and set the water beside you. Place your palms together and, keeping the fingers straight, rub the palms together in a circular motion for approximately half a minute.

Take up the glass and hold it against the solar plexus with both hands, fingertips and thumbs touching (your solar plexus is just above your navel). Take deep breaths and concentrate towards the water. Visualise the colour blue. Hold your head comfortably; your eyes can be open or closed. Empty your mind of all except the water and the colour. After two minutes, drink one-third of the water.

Now take some more deep breaths while seated and return to the palm circling once more.

Repeat the exercise twice, until all the water is drunk. This exercise also aids concentration. Some of your personal energy will be transferred to the water, which will become your focus point. Your mind, your hands and your solar plexus, are engaged in actually generating energy: energy that you will drink in the revitalised water. The water becomes an energising tonic.

When you feel ready, over a period of time, gradually increase the time of focus from two to five minutes.

This exercise is so beneficial you should make it part of your day and look forward to treating yourself with these few minutes to relax and revitalise.

> *Start tomorrow as a positive day.*
>
> *Make sure that in no way do you contribute to the suffering or misery of another human being and that in some way, however small, you end the day having lessened the burden for someone else, with a kind word of praise or encouragement, a warm smile or an act of compassion.*

REVIVE

This exercise is useful when you feel tired and need extra energy. It can be done anywhere and will always help when you cannot have a rest immediately.

Bring together the thumb and first two fingers of the right hand, and then press these fingers into the hollow at the base of the skull, at the back of the neck. This is the occipital region of the brain. Pressing the fingers firmly but gently, take a deep breath and hold it as long as convenient, then slowly exhale. Repeat this exercise a few times.

This exercise causes a discharge of excess energy. This energy then goes through the radial nerves to the fingertips and is transmitted to the occipital region. The energy is then further transmitted to the spinal nervous system and eases tension.

> *Take time to think - it is the source of power.*
> *Take time to be friendly - it is the road to happiness.*
> *Take time to laugh - it is the music of the soul.*
> *Take time to play - it is the secret of perpetual youth.*

MEDITATIONAL
THOUGHTS

Faced with the most terrifying and final of circumstances with time to make contact with their family and friends; the only message that human beings wish to send is one of love. Through love you can merge in the ocean of love. Love cures pettiness, hate and grief and loosens bonds. It saves people from the torment of death. Love binds all hearts in a soft harmony. Seen through the eyes of love, all beings are beautiful, all deeds are dedicated and all thoughts are innocent; the world is one vast family. Love can tame even the most ferocious of beasts. Start pouring out love to all members of your community and gradually expand that love to include all mankind, and then even the lower creatures.

Soak every moment in love. Be born in love, live in love and die in love. Be a wave in the ocean of love. Cultivate love, tolerance, humility, faith and reverence. Spread love, be full of love.

Love must see the best in others and not the worst; Love cannot ignore the divinity in others. Love is the basis of character and is the greatest virtue.

> *Love changes everything,*
> *the way we think,*
> *the way we live,*
> *the way we die.*

THE CELESTIAL
FOUNTAIN MEDITATION

When you are meditating in your usual place, imagine there is a door opposite you. Imagine you are opening the door. Beyond it is a place of great beauty. There are prisms of light. All the colours of the rainbow are dancing around you and this is accompanied by a delicate tinkling sound that for a moment you could believe there is a crystal chandelier gently moving in a breeze and that sunlight reflected through it is creating the colours around you.

Then you see it is not a chandelier but a fountain of crystal clear water with no visible source, just a circle of pure water falling down, reflecting light through it, and creating the myriad of colours around you. You walk towards it and step into the fountain and the water falls on you, so very gently, in droplets. It refreshes and cleanses you. All parts of you are invigorated; all sorrows and disappointments are washed away from you.

When you are ready leave this place. Gently close the door. Return whenever you feel you need to.

> *Where there is hatred let me sow love*
> *Where there is injury, pardon;*
> *Where there is doubt, faith;*
> *Where there is darkness, light;*
> *Where there is despair, hope and*
> *Where there is sadness, joy.*

ASPIRATION

To aspire is to desire earnestly. Why not desire a better more fulfilled life? We desire enough things that can harm us so why not desire good things that will help us?

Following this workbook will have been an opportunity to discover yourself. To shed burdens that hold you back and to understand human nature, by understanding yourself. Having greater compassion, a better view and knowing what motivates you will enable you to achieve goals that until now seemed out of reach.

By meditating you will eventually achieve higher consciousness. Developing your spirituality will enable you to forgive people who respond to you in a negative way and hurt you. Allowing you to see, perhaps for the first time, that someone who is hostile, hurtful, or aggressive, is probably someone who has, or is, experiencing these emotions themselves. They are permanently on guard in their dealings with others and cannot easily display trust or warmth. It is natural to be angry sometimes, life is difficult and challenging, it contains many painful experiences and dilemmas. Understanding the importance of insight, using it to avoid fuelling or sustaining anger over long periods will prevent the anger from eating into the fabric of your being. Automatically releasing reserves of energy that you can use to reach the goals that you aspire to.

Absolutely everyone is entitled to aspire to something. It might be that you want to be fitter, lose weight, be more successful at work, start your own business, or become actively involved in a charity. These plans and schemes sit at the back of our minds waiting for us to bring them to fruition. One day, hopefully we will. Sadly, if we don't, if the schemes are shelved, it can lead to frustration and regret in later life. Holistically, it is important not only to have plans and dreams but also to realistically assess when and how they might be achieved. To have unfulfilled ambitions that have not been realised will affect your mind, body and spirit adversely in the future.

The first thing is to identify your goal or goals. Just working through the sections may have prompted you to remember something you always thought you would like to do, but never got round to. Perhaps by identifying your favourite subjects at school you have thought more seriously about taking them to a higher level of competence, perhaps even changing your career direction. Only you know what you would like to achieve.

Obviously it is important to marry up your skills with your aspirations. It is not possible to achieve certain things if you cannot gain the abilities needed. This is not an excuse, it is a fact, a distinction you need to recognise and accept if you are going to succeed. When thinking about your skills, remember all the positive comments people have made about you in the past. This does not have to be an overblown egotistical view of yourself in which you attribute some stunning, if inaccurate abilities, to your self-image. Nor should it be that of a shrinking violet, afraid to lay claim to real virtues, abilities and skills. It should be an accurate appraisal that will help you see your strengths and weaknesses realistically.

Now you have begun to think about yourself in a holistic way you will be able to do this. You will also know that all the aspects of yourself are equally important if you are to succeed. When you an integrated whole, Mind, Body and Spirit in harmony you will become the driver of your vehicle and not merely the passenger.

Aspiration will prevent you from gravitating to the lowest denominator. Aspiration can help you reach your goals; it can also help you rise up out of any adverse situation. You can use it to create a ladder to get you up the most slippery of slopes and to establish yourself, firmly, back in the running. It can help you reach goals you may have thought impossible and enable you to develop yourself to the absolute zenith of your ability.

After you have been living holistically for twelve weeks look at the answers and questions again. You may find your perception has changed and you are able to put your life, your experiences, hopes and aspirations into better perspective.

Achieve whatever you desire, now. Begin to harness your life force by starting each day with this positive thought. Look at yourself in the bathroom mirror.

You are not going to leave your day to chance; you are going to give your subconscious mind an order. You are going to feed it with the thoughts and vibrations of your choice. Choose the kind of day you want to live. For instance, if you want to smoke or eat less or be more positive, concentrate on telling this to your subconscious mind. When you feel you have done this sufficiently, dismiss all thoughts from your mind and relax. Then after a few minutes go about your daily life.

For further information about our one-day and residential courses
and our corporate division 'DAEDALUS' contact

MOSS HILL HOLISTIC CENTRE
BETWS-Y-COED
NORTH WALES
LL24 0PW

Telephone: 01690 710198   Fax: 01690 710907

www.holisticsolutions.co.uk

**Published in Great Britain by the
Aquarius Book Agency
Registered 9.1.81**